Finding the Boyfriend Within
Zombie 00
Godtalk
City Poet
The Golden Age of Promiscuity
Scary Kisses

Dating
the
Greek Gods

Empowering Spiritual Messages
on Sex and Love, Creativity and Wisdom

BRAD GOOCH

Simon & Schuster

NEW YORK LONDON TORONTO SYDNEY SINGAPORE

SIMON & SCHUSTER
Rockefeller Center
1230 Avenue of the Americas
New York, NY 10020

SIMON & SCHUSTER and colophon are
registered trademarks of Simon & Schuster, Inc.

For information about special discounts for bulk purchases,
please contact Simon & Schuster Special Sales at
1-800-456-6798 or business@simonandschuster.com

Manufactured in the United States of America

1   3   5   7   9   10   8   6   4   2

Library of Congress Cataloging-in-Publication Data
Gooch, Brad, date.
Dating the Greek gods : empowering spiritual messages on
sex and love, creativity and wisdom / Brad Gooch.
p. cm.
1. Mythology, Greek—Miscellanea. 2. Gay men. I. Title.

BL785.G63 2003
292.2'113—dc21   2003043217

ISBN 0-7432-2669-0

ACKNOWLEDGMENTS

Special thanks to: my editor Chuck Adams; my agent, Joy Harris; my friend Barbara Heizer for creative suggestions as she read this book in manuscript; and Michael Selleck at Simon & Schuster for his inspiring support. For other epiphanies along the way, I wish to thank: Tasos Pappas, Paul Raushenbush, Derrick Smit, and Diane von Furstenberg.

To Michael Scalisi

CONTENTS

INTRODUCTION

Soon after my fiftieth birthday, a metamorphosis occurred: I began dating Greek gods. Not those elusive objects of our affection, "Greek gods" in quotation marks, but *the* Greek gods, of ancient mythology. By spending quality time—a process I thought of as "dating"—trying to get to know more intimately the principles, characteristics, and powers ascribed to the classical deities, I approached the much-touted literature of the Greeks as an open invitation rather than a literary cliché.

Simultaneously that spring, I did begin dating guys again, too—the human kind, who saunter around Manhattan in cargo pants and sleek blue sunglasses, and give you their cell phone number while waiting for a traffic light to change at a street corner. For a long time, I'd felt too old or too advanced to indulge in anything as adolescent as dating. When the topic came up, I'd dismiss dates as "job interviews in disguise" or "an entry-level position in life."

Asking questions and formulating answers grew in tandem

with openness to the notion of two mature adults going on a date. Dating turned out to be no longer necessarily a virtual page torn from a 1950s Archie and Veronica comic book. As much philosophizing as flirting can transpire on a date. Certainly the conversations on my own dates have done much to further my attempts at growing in wisdom. And wisdom, it turns out, can be sexy. As soon as someone revealed to me that he was reading a book titled *If the Buddha Dated,* I saw his unshaved face as suddenly far more textured.

Dating the Greek Gods is a journal of those dates—both the human and the divine. The chapters are devoted to the dominant traits of the gods of the pantheon: Apollo, the god of wisdom; Dionysus, sensuality; Hermes, communication; Hephaestus, creativity; Eros, love; and Zeus, power. The last chapter will shift from mythology to address the philosophical soul that evolved from this ancient Greek spirituality—the inner voice of the philosopher Socrates, which he called his Inner Oracle. Included are meditations on the gods' abstract qualities, with enough deep gossip from my own experiences, I confess, to keep this book ever bordering on memoir. Included as well are a series of suggestions for exercises that may lead you to your own epiphanies (from the Greek word meaning "an appearance or manifestation of a deity").

I was encouraged to think of delving into the wisdom of Apollo or the energy of Dionysus as dating, counterintuitively, by a friend who's pastor of a high-profile Christian church. (Glinting in his past are three silver Junior Olympics medals in swimming.) Pastor Bob wrote me a bingo of an e-mail on the concept: "I think the terminology of 'dating' is an intriguing way of entering into spiritual exploration. What does dating mean if not making ourselves vulnerable with at least the possibility of being transformed into more than we were?"

Last week, my computer-geek friend, Eric, pedaled up curbside on his mountain bike. He has managed to conjure more trouble in his thirty-five years than most. Eric finds himself teetering now on step ten of a twelve-step ladder of recovery. Besides our burning debate on Mac versus Windows, we'd been discussing my own dates with the Greek gods. I'd been telling him of my attempts to find relevance for Apollonian wisdom and clear thought in my romantic life. That afternoon Eric admitted he'd been flirting with a relationship that had many of the warning signs of disasters past. This time, however, he confronted the accident waiting to happen up front.

"I realized I had to listen to my Apollo," he said brightly.

Eric's personal inventory had given him newly discovered powers for dealing with life's gods and monsters. And my own tales of dates with Greek gods had given us a language in which to quickly telegraph wisdom to each other in a fashion both poetic and practical.

There's a backstory to the origins of this book. One of my hats is professor of English at William Paterson University, in New Jersey—State U, as I shorten it for friends. And one of my regular courses is Western Literature to the Renaissance, involving readings in translation of ancient Greek and Roman classics. The kids are predominantly Italian-American from northern New Jersey, and most have more pressing preoccupations than mythology. But one semester, fate threw me a fish in the guise of a group of uncharacteristically interested students.

To them I owe thanks for the first glimmerings of seeing in these gilded texts not just poetry, history, propaganda, and entertainment, but also helpful messages—self-help . . . *literary self-help.*

(Another inspiration was Alain de Botton's witty and casually edifying *How Proust Can Change Your Life,* one of the few books on the shelf that bends genres by discovering life lessons in the unlikely source of a literary masterpiece—in his case, Marcel Proust's twentieth-century French novel *Remembrance of Things Past.*)

One evening early in the semester, I'd written the term EPIPHANY on the board with a nub of white chalk. I ticked off many of the epiphanies in Homer's epic poems, the *Iliad* and the *Odyssey,* when gods appear to warriors and cause them to make a right turn rather than a left, or to blossom in some unexpected fashion. For instance, when Odysseus is languishing in the seductive Calypso's cave, their one-night stand threatening to stretch into eternity, Hermes, the messenger of the gods—accessorized with wings on his ankles—arrives to get our hero moving again back to home and family:

> *No words were lost on Hermes, the Wayfinder,*
> *Who bent to tie his beautiful sandals on,*
> *ambrosial, golden, that carry him over water*
> *or over endless land in a swish of the wind,*
> *and took the wand with which he charms asleep—*
> *or when he will, awake—the eyes of men.*
> *So wand in hand he paced into the air.*
>
> (FITZGERALD TRANSLATION)

"That's an epiphany," I said. "It's a Greek version of psychology. Odysseus isn't just about to meet a god. A lightbulb is going off in his head. He's depressed, and he's suddenly going to feel empowered to change his life, to get moving."

Cut to: the parking lot.

Under the darkness of the new moon, I was making my way after class through lines of shadowy pickup trucks, SUVs, and Mustang convertibles when I was suddenly joined by Frank, a cheerful enough guy with an outdoorsy beard and a gut that protruded through his overflowing Van Morrison T-shirt. Frank seemed older than most of the other students . . . maybe late twenties. His hand would shoot up with comments and questions trimmed with references to the Nets basketball team, Mets baseball team, or the Jets football team. On this walk, though, he dropped all such athletic references.

"That was cool, what you said about the god thing being like human psychology . . . like a larger-than-life thing."

"Why thanks, Frank," I replied, admittedly attracted by the timbre of his voice and our sudden intimacy.

"Do you think it's like coming out? Like the voice that told you to come out?"

"What do you mean, Frank?" I asked, shifting my overstuffed book bag awkwardly on my shoulder.

"Well, I'm gay—but I haven't come out to hardly anybody."

Startled, I asked, "You're gay?" I was accustomed to being able to size up such inclinations. But here my tracking system had obviously failed entirely.

"Yup," he said, clearly enjoying the joke of having stumped even me.

"And so you think being gay is like some gay Hermes with winged feet flying down from Mount Olympus and tapping you on the head?"

"Felt that way to me. . . . I sure didn't think it up."

Trying to recoup a few points, I segued into corny advice-column banter about getting counseling from a gay hot line, suggesting various gay websites, perhaps even a visit to a local bar.

"I've been to Feathers, but that's just what the guys look like there—feathers. . . . I'm more into bears."

"Oh."

On the drive back to the city, alone in a car pool backseat while my two colleagues up front discussed an English department meeting, I kept thinking back to Frank . . . Frank and Hermes.

Certainly the message to "Come out" was the best analogy I'd heard to the manner in which larger-than-life deities would sweep in and out of the lives of the ancient heroes, whispering in the ear of their souls. I wondered if there were other implications. If reading these poems from over twenty-five hundred years ago could be relevant to Frank's sexuality, they might be relevant to other critical life issues as well.

Not only was I a tweedy English professor at the time, I was also the author of *Finding the Boyfriend Within*. Somehow that book, written a couple of years earlier, primed me to begin looking at these extinct gods in a more lively way.

The premise of *Finding the Boyfriend Within* was simply that happiness, well-being, and a sense of purpose come from within, that too often we imagine that someone has to come along to validate our existential parking ticket. The book's motto might well have been "Be your own boyfriend."

Ever since its publication, I'd been asked, challengingly, "So, did you find your Boyfriend Within?"

My perennial answer: "Sure."

By regularly checking with my Voice Within—a technique, outlined in that book, for carrying on a dialogue with an inner guiding voice—and by scheduling dates with myself (the book's essential exercise), I felt reasonably balanced. The question was where to go next. Many readers believed the obvious destination was a boyfriend—that the sequel would be *The Boyfriend Within Meets the Boyfriend Without*. On book tour, a hand would inevitably shoot up after a lively Q&A with the show-stopping question "But if I read your book and do all the exercises . . . *then* will I get a boyfriend?"

If anything was hidden between the lines of *Boyfriend Within*, a husband-hunting manual was less apparent to me than a medieval spiritual treatise. Certainly the question posed in its final chapter, "What's love got to do with it?" and the answer, "Love is the selfless work you do for another. Love makes you feel loved," hark back to a traditional scriptural message. The book's conclusion, borrowed from Rumi, the medieval Sufi poet who transposed his longing for reunion with his friend Shams into love poems of longing for God, was transmitting a spiritual, if not mystical, message: "Lovers don't finally meet somewhere / They're in each other all along."

I thought the direction I was sailing toward was "gay spirituality." During the summers of 2000 and 2002, I sent up two trial balloons by teaching seminars on "Spiritual Buddies" at Esalen

Institute in Big Sur. Yet I always felt uncomfortable using the buzzword "spiritual." Pulling from the vast files of tradition was helpful, but I was shadowed by the knowledge that gays had been burned by all the world's great religions. To embrace their rituals without the politics had an air of "Don't ask, don't tell." I wondered how to be able to discuss the interior life without all the baggage.

In exploring the Greek gods, I began to breathe a more neutral air. These were gods who had been defrocked. (Well, except for Dionysus, who cross-dresses.) I also began to realize that they weren't offering spirituality with a scent of otherworldliness. They were offering wisdom. The very ecology of the pantheon seemed worldly-wise in its balance of light and dark, conflict and peace, sexuality and spirituality. Many of the gods were bisexual. (Zeus was in love with the Trojan prince Ganymede, aka Aquarius, who became his cupbearer; Apollo with Hyacinthus.) Some, though, were badly in need of anger therapy. I admit to my own politically correct loss of nerve by not including Ares, the testosterone-driven god of war. But then, even Homer, the source of most of our stories of the gods, mostly ignored Ares, and the peace-loving Athenians never built him a temple.

When I arrived in Manhattan in the early 1970s, lots of young, liberated types were roaming the streets. Utopianism was in the air as gender politics promised a less repressive future. Promiscuity was given content by political purpose. And much self-mythologizing went on. Everyone seemed to be making himself up as he went along, actually wearing motorcycle jackets, logger boots, and cowboy boots borrowed from the closets of mythic archetypes. Within two decades, many of

these free spirits were dead of AIDS-related diseases. I've often thought, if they were still around, what ancient mariners they'd be, with tales to tell. I know that *Finding the Boyfriend Within* was partly a response to the death, in 1989, of my lover of eleven years from "the plague." Likewise, *Dating the Greek Gods* is partly a substitute for imaginary conversations that might have been with so many of those potential and potentially wise comrades—a self-reliant attempt to put experience together with meaning, with as light a touch as possible.

When *Finding the Boyfriend Within* was released, its readership, to my surprise, included more than gay men. A few women came up to me after readings and claimed the book spoke to their own questions. I was invited to be a guest on a sports radio show in Philadelphia, where I addressed mostly straight men about the cliché of the unkempt bachelor pad as a symptom of low self-image. A recently divorced reporter from Fort Lauderdale called me after our newspaper interview, wondering if the book could help him through his transition, basically asking for permission to read it. Certainly, among the Greek gods are role models for every anagram of gender and gender role.

Wisdom can push the refresh button on identity. What follows is a series of opportunities to confront some of the bigger questions of sexuality, community, creativity, and love as personified in the Greek gods. A week spent with each god might be most productive. (If not now, when?) There is logic to the order in which they appear. However, the book could always be read straight through in one stretch. Each chapter includes a profile of a god, a series of exercises for engaging with his prime qualities, and a culminating date. Whichever way they are ap-

proached, a result of brushes with gods may be transformation, or as the Roman poet Ovid called them, metamorphoses. It's never too late to morph.

In the classical literature, gods and goddesses often appear in human disguise. When Athena is in the guise of a soldier armed with a spear, she has a heart-to-heart with Odysseus's son, Telemachus—basically telling him to grow up. This book is full of thoughts and exercises involving dating or social life. If the exercises are worked through, the world can begin to seem a more mythic place, where significant messages are being sent and received by people all the time, and where destiny is a game being played out, complete with clues. I admitted that during the process I found myself dating again—I'm not sure which was cause and which effect. If you notice an escalation in dating in your life—with new acquaintances, friends, or long-time partners—go for it.

Socrates taught that "the unexamined life is not worth living." The motto for this book might well be the bumper sticker of a divine command from which he borrowed that sentiment, engraved over the temple of Apollo in Delphi: KNOW THYSELF.

One

APOLLO
THE GOD OF WISDOM

PROFILE

Apollo is the Mr. Right of the Greek pantheon. A son of almighty Zeus, the king of the gods, and one of Zeus's many mistresses—the lovely Leto—Apollo is generally described as tall, dark, and handsome. A Homeric hymn to Apollo tells us that when the young god with his long, curling black hair first appeared on Mount Olympus and drew his bow, all the gods and goddesses rose from their seats in astonishment.

Gazing at a marble frieze of the gods and goddesses making up the pantheon, Nietzsche, the German philosopher and classicist, wrote of Apollo's special star quality: "We must not be misled by the fact that Apollo stands side by side with the others as an individual deity, without any claim to priority of rank. For the same impulse that embodies itself in Apollo gave birth to this entire Olympian world, and in this sense Apollo is its father."

Apollo was a player. His love life was protean, but his success with women wasn't as stellar as might be expected. Daphne had herself transformed into a laurel tree to escape his advances. Afterward, Apollo would wear a branch of laurel as a wreath on his head—hence, as he was also the god of poetry, the phrase "poet laureate." When Cassandra remained unimpressed by his attributes, he cursed her with the gift of prophecy, which included a caveat that no one would ever believe her accurate warnings about the future.

He had more luck with handsome young men, whose love for him was at least reciprocal. Yet these romances ended tragically as well. Apollo's great infatuation was Hyacinthus, a divine boy who rode swans instead of horses. Apollo would carry the nets when Hyacinthus went fishing, lead the dogs when he went hunting, and accompany him on hiking trips into the mountains, while neglecting his own practice of the lyre and archery. One day when Hyacinthus and Apollo were throwing the discus, the wind was shifted by the jealous west wind, Zephyrus, who was also in love with the boy. The discus sliced Hyacinthus through the skull. From the drops of his purple blood grew the hyacinth flower.

Apollo's next infatuation, Cyparissus, accidentally speared his own pet stag, a flashy sports car of a creature with gilded antlers and festooned with silver ornaments. Cyparissus was so inconsolable when he discovered his misfire that Apollo turned him into a sorrowing tree, the cypress, an evergreen often planted in cemeteries. For these passionate affairs, Apollo is distinguished as the first god to woo someone of the same sex. He might well be nominated on that basis for the vacant post of god of homosexuality. (In Greek legend, the first mortal to pursue another man was the poet Thamyris, who was also in love with Hyacinthus.)

But Nietzsche didn't single out Apollo as the trophy god because he scored sporadically with young beauties of either sex. As with mortals, a disconnect can exist between a god's love life and his work life. Apollo could be dizzy when he was in pursuit of a long redial list of potential lovers. But when he was at the office, he was all business. His focus was sustained and steady. During the workday, Apollo was the sun, and so his job was the spreading of light. His arc was perfection itself. No quality was finally more crucial for energizing Olympian spirituality than light. As the god of the sun, he was, by extension, the god of all things positive, life-giving, and full of clarity. His light was spiritual as well as solar.

Apollo exhausted many fields in his endeavors as a deity. Exhibiting symptoms resembling attention deficit disorder, he was the god of prophecy, healing and medicine, poetry, music, philosophy, astronomy, archery, youth, wisdom, beauty, intelligence, and moderation. The transformation of so many of his lovers into trees and flowers reveals his closeness with nature. But shooting through all these manifestations is the principle of light. "Light" is the root word in "enlightenment." Hidden in "enlightenment" is the sense of lightening up. His style of music and poetry is likewise illuminating. His mode was never heavy metal. He was much more classical.

The most famous of all the ancient temples was Apollo's temple at Delphi, believed by the Greeks to be the center of the world, its exact site marked with a large conical stone, the *omphalos,* or navel. The two guiding principles engraved on the temple in the sixth century B.C. were KNOW THYSELF and ALL

THINGS IN MODERATION. (Both commands were later accepted by the Greek philosophers Socrates, Plato, and Aristotle as the basis of morality.) The light of wisdom that produces intuition and healing balance is the shining logo of the Olympian brand. The Athenian Greeks roved freely through all experience in their integration of life with wisdom. They didn't leave any dark closets in their psyches unexposed. But even at their most garish and violent, they maintained a glow of sanity about them. This glow was the halo of the Apollonian principle of wisdom.

MEDITATIONS AND EXERCISES
STREET WISDOM

Apollo's wisdom can sound like the most abstract of principles, the most far-off and Olympian. The Greek word for wisdom, *sophia,* possesses some lofty connotations. The early Greek-speaking Christians even identified the word with Jesus Christ, as the wisdom of God. (Hence Hagia Sophia, or Holy Wisdom, was the soaring Byzantine church in Istanbul.)

But *sophia* in ancient Greek had more practical definitions, too. The word could denote skill, craft, cleverness, know-how, cunning, smartness, even expedience. These meanings are closer to our own sense of "streetwise."

The best way to extract wisdom with a capital *W* from our street experiences is to practice formulating what we've learned—to exercise wisdom. The most productive place to start is with our relationships past and present. We grow wise from our relationships. Nothing speeds up the process of wisdom more than passion—whether sexual, romantic, or deriving from a deep friendship. Wisdom isn't a purely intellectual quality. The Greek goddess Psyche—her name means "Soul"—was in love, after all, with Eros, the god of romantic love. The soul needs juice from which to distill wisdom.

APOLLONIAN EXERCISE #1

List significant relationships that you've had in your life: trysts, friends, lovers, or partners. Try for five. Then write down lessons you have learned about yourself and life from these relationships.

Each of us has his own quotient of wisdom gained from a personal supply of experiences. I'm going to share my findings. Hopefully, these results will resonate with yours, but you will certainly have conclusions that are entirely your own. Depending on how our particular hand of cards is dealt, we arrive at different insights in different orders and at different times.

My list:

- Sally
- Howard
- Dirk
- The Boyfriend Within
- The two Larrys

Sally and I began our romance in college. I was already experimenting with guys. But the comfort of bubble baths and nights shared with her under a patchwork quilt made for an invaluable home base. Yet Dionysus, the god of sexual energy, soon demanded his due.

Lesson: I was gay.

Howard was a lucky stumble into love. This eleven-year relationship had many of the traits I've since come to think of as wise for the long term, but didn't even know I was looking for at the time.

Lesson: Shared interests, parity of mind and body, and brotherly love all contribute to long-lasting relationships.

Dirk, with his long black hair and heavy Southern accent, resembled Apollo. (Although he didn't *sound* like Apollo.) He told me everything I wanted to hear: "I'm the one you've been waiting for." Six months later, he eloped with a plastic surgeon.

Lesson: "If it sounds too good to be true, it usually is." (Borrowed from an online-profile quotation, a great source of folk wisdom.)

If your lessons begin sounding disgruntled, like mine directly above, another bit of wisdom found online is useful: "Don't judge others, evaluate yourself."

The Boyfriend Within, after our two years of dating, left me much lighter, happier, and more relaxed. Much of what passes for love and romance is disguised insecurity.

Lesson: Happiness comes from within. By going within, you mysteriously get outside yourself.

The two Larrys, with whom I recently experienced romantic sparks, are two of my longtime friends, one on the East Coast, the other on the West. For over a decade, I'd found both to be stimulating company. In both cases, we just went to the next step: sleepovers.

Lesson: Having demythologized obsessive love in time spent with the Boyfriend Within, I now find certain friendships to be more passionate affairs.

During the early 1980s, I was employed as the porn critic for the *New York Native,* a now-defunct gay newspaper. My beat was the Adonis movie theater, a baroque pile in midtown Manhattan long since demolished. While taking notes on a mangled little pad, I would often drift from appraising the antics on-screen to staring through the living lust of shadows of men traipsing up and down the center aisle.

One evening I found myself in the singular position of weeping as the credits rolled at the end of a film: Tom de Simone's *The Idol*. This prevideo production began with an unlikely (for porn) sequence in which we witness the death in a car accident of the main character, a golden high school idol of a track star, very much Apollo's type. The conceit was that we were at grave-side and given access to the heads of each of the mourners as they replayed their memories of the deceased. The first romantic interest, acted by a transvestite, was his girlfriend, with whom he made out in the backseat of a car. She was followed by the coach, who massaged his star athlete in an overly attentive manner following an injury. Next was a teammate who had joined him in a masturbation duet in the shower.

Eventually the camera circled upward to reveal a boy on his bicycle, surveying the burial from an overlook. Entering into his brunette head, we found that he and the track star had been boyfriends. The "idol" had progressed in his sentimental education through more and more authentic liaisons, discovering simultaneously his sexuality and his capacity for love. Together these two cavorted in a swimming pool, and then on a king-size mattress in an anonymous bedroom while the sound track "Love Is in the Air" played like aural soap bubbles. At the film's conclusion, with the bereft boyfriend leaning against what might as well have been a cypress, the lesson of love had been imparted.

This film could be exhibit A in street wisdom. Through its mixture of sexuality, romance, love, and death, a spiral is set in motion that illustrates how lessons learned from relationships eventually allow the main character to find love and identity. Without the disco music and mythological dye jobs, our own lives can follow just such a spiral if we grow in wisdom through our experiences. If we don't assimilate wisdom, then we will repeat ourselves, and our lives will likely remain a revolving circle.

INTUITIVE WISDOM

Apollo was big box office in the ancient world mostly because of his association with prophecy.

He was said to have learned the art of prophecy at a very young age. Gods grew quite fast, so he might have been just a few weeks old. By the time he was four days old, after all, he had already killed the dragon Python with his bow and arrow in the temple of Delphi, which at that time was still the temple of the earth mother, Gaia. Apollo's teacher in prophecy was Pan, a goat-legged god on the island of Crete. Importing this gift to his oracle at Delphi, who chewed a leaf of Apollo's bay laurel during her oracular trances, he became so identified with prophecy that most soothsayers claimed some connection to him.

The ancients were as titillated as we are by hearing prophecies of the future. They delighted in many varieties of sortilege, or divination, including the reading of entrails of birds. Lots of popular contemporary activities are their descendants: Ouija boards, tarot cards, horoscopes, I Ching, runes, palm reading, and crystal balls.

Skill in all of these activities could be filed under prophetic intuition. The forms of intuition that continue to amaze are such bright tricks as predicting the future or having psychic abilities. A friend swore to me that he'd been playing a game of guessing unseen cards from a pile with a partner and became so expert as the night wore on that the partner insisted on stopping, claiming to be spooked by his ability. Another friend uncharacteristically turned off her computer before leaving her loft one summer morning, thinking to herself that there would be a power failure. An hour later a Con Edison substation exploded and all Lower Manhattan lost electrical power. (In her case, though, her downstairs neighbor had commented the day before on brownouts. Many cases of psychic foreshadowing involve just such a dose of knowledge subtly assimilated.)

More transformative, if less flashy, is the application of intuition in daily life. Intuitions are basically felt thoughts. They don't arrive as actual verbal messages. They arrive more in a form such as "I have a good feeling about that guy." Some people are more intuitive than others. Or perhaps some simply have practiced more—like the friend with the playing cards. "I think people who have good intuitions tend not to be as needy," a friend recently conjectured between puffs of a late-night cigarette. "It means being open . . . being able to read the tea leaves. Being able to look at what's there even if it doesn't conform to what you want to be there . . . even if it doesn't feed your ego. You have to be able to face down your fears to be truly intuitive."

His theory sounded good to me. But theory bought or not, intuition can be tested until you discover its benefits. Gods and goddesses come with attributes, like superheroes, and with props that symbolize those attributes. Apollo's wreath of bay laurel marks him as a poet and a champion athlete—victorious athletes were graced with a crown of laurel for winning competitions—but also as one gifted with good prophetic intuitions. Such an Apollonian gift can be developed and tested in the interpersonal world.

APOLLONIAN EXERCISE #2

List friends and acquaintances who elicit a positive feeling. Then list those who elicit a negative feeling. Over the next week, spend time only with those on the positive list.

The premise behind this exercise is that your intuitions, if followed, will change your life for the better. You already have a built-in monitor that will guide you more wisely than any oracle or guru. Crucial to benefiting from this exercise is being able to identify a positive feeling about someone. This skill might sound obvious. But too often our sense of positive feeling becomes garbled on its way from the gut through the heart to the brain. We have lots of contradictory impulses and agendas. The simple feel-good message is intercepted along the way. Having a positive feeling about someone simply means that when you conjure up their name or image you feel comfortable, stress-free, or happy.

Being skilled at recognizing a positive feeling requires being in touch with your body. I was told by an ex-disciple of the Hindu leader Maharishi Mahesh Yogi (who famously appeared on the cover of the *Sgt. Pepper's Lonely Hearts Club Band* album) that followers would sit with him and pose long, complex questions about what they should do with their lives. His usual simple response: "Feel your body!" If you're having trouble identifying your feelings about someone, just tune in to any physical sensations you have while thinking of them—tiredness, anxiety, or boredom.

My own positive list included half a dozen of the usual suspects among my friends. On the negative side, three or four I avoided. But I also found, on the negative list, Jeff. Now here was a tough one because Jeff is a creative director in an advertising firm who's helped me get work and make some solid connections. But it's true that he always suggests a dinner, and the dinner is barely over before he's suggested another, no matter how unsatisfying the first. I'm stumped at his motives and consistency.

Nevertheless, Jeff is stimulating enough, and there is the business angle. I do enjoy him well enough in small doses. When I wanted to have a clear week of responsible social life, full of good feeling, the first thing I did was call Jeff up to make a dinner date . . . for the following week. I'd removed the obligatory dinner from my schedule and my mind. But cowardly lion that I am, I hadn't chosen a radical free fall from all such obligations.

This exercise takes some practice because you may find—as did I—one or two friends on the negative-feeling list. Life is complex enough that having some friends about whom you have ambivalent feelings is fine. And giving of time selflessly to someone in need—whether stimulating company or not—is more than fine. If you continue to do this exercise over time, though, your list might shift. This exercise can be gradually expanded to include more activities. Begin exploring your intuitions with lists. Then try putting them into practice for a week. You'll start feeling freer and communicating that sense without trying. You'll cultivate the air of someone on permanent vacation.

Another opportunity for Apollonian intuition is deciding what to do at night. Again there are certain restaurants or bars about which you have a positive feeling. If you spend a week visiting only those spots and staying away from others, you'll experience the same lightening up as with the list of friends. Also, people and locations can hop lists. One night you might have a completely negative feeling about going to a certain club. But a month later you might have a positive feeling about the same establishment. Listen to those messages. They are a reliable navigating device. This approach saves you the trouble of making too many ultimatums and decisions from which you later stray.

Intuition about career choices can be critical and have the most obvious long-term consequences. I once offered, unsolicited, to a friend the intuition that he'd make a good screenwriter. Three scripts later, he's on his way. But our surest intuitions concern ourselves. We have a more complete emotional and biographical dossier on ourselves, and good intuition often involves such prior knowledge and information. If you're at a career intersection, try writing down a list of jobs or projects about which you have a positive feeling and those about which you have a negative feeling. You might be surprised at the outcome. Try following through on looking for a different job, or beginning a new career or project. But don't quit your day job immediately based on the results.

Our intuition is ultimately our guide through life. I once sat in the back of a car careening down the wrong road somewhere in the Lake District in England. In the front seat was my favorite husband-and-wife couple. She was fumbling with a map that seemed larger than the entire dashboard, trying to distinguish tiny red lines from blue in order to rescue us from an increasingly puzzling terrain, full of cows. Realizing that her suggestions were only making matters worse, the husband snapped, "Don't listen to Jane. She doesn't have any sense of direction." "My dear," she responded elegantly, without missing a beat, "I've guided you through life." Everyone laughed at the truth of the perception.

While not all of us might be so fortunate as to have such a wife, we all do have the possibility of having just such a reliable guide through life in our Apollonian intuition. If we have trained our intuition to be healthy, to gravitate toward happiness and the light, we will always have this homing device. If we stay true to our Apollonian principle when faced with decisions such as those about relationships, or whether or not to adopt children, or what project to undertake next, or what religion to practice, or how best to spend our vacations—all the big stuff— we're likely to wind up with the destiny best suited for our character. Our life will be a relaxed fit rather than an awkward squeeze.

WISDOM AND BALANCE

Apollo's signature statement was "Everything in moderation," also translated as "Nothing in excess." The enemy of barbarism, he stood for moderation in all things. The seven strings of his guitarlike instrument, the lute, were connected with the seven vowels of the later Greek alphabet and used for therapeutic music. At the end of the first book of the *Iliad*, Apollo is found strumming soothingly for the gods at twilight, with backup from the Muses, the female goddesses who inspire all the arts:

> *Thus thereafter the whole long day until the sun went under*
> *they feasted, nor was anyone's hunger denied a fair portion,*
> *nor denied the beautifully wrought lyre in the hands of Apollo*
> *nor the antiphonal sweet sound of the Muses singing.*
>
> (LATTIMORE TRANSLATION)

Balance and moderation heal. This connection can jive Apollo's quality of balance with his role as a healer and god of medicine. Like Walt Whitman on the battlefields of the Civil War, Apollo is often pictured in the *Iliad* as a nurse mending wounded soldiers—especially those of his favored side, the Trojans. When the warrior Glaucus prays to him on the battlefield of Troy,

> *. . . . Phoibos Apollo heard him.*
> *At once he made the pains stop, and dried away from the hard wound*
> *the dark running of blood, and put strength into his spirit.*
>
> (LATTIMORE TRANSLATION)

Apollo was as balanced as the classical architecture of his own temples. For the Greeks, this principle was the foundation of morality. Such a notion might seem odd, or subversive. We're used to thinking of moral choices in terms of right and wrong, good and evil, black and white. The Apollonian principle is that all actions need to be balanced by other actions.

APOLLONIAN EXERCISE #3

For a week, keep track of the number of hours you spend doing different activities, such as sleeping, working, or watching TV. At the end of the week, draw up a balance sheet. Based on your own goals, try to adjust any imbalances the following week.

I've given this exercise to students. Usually the big shock is how few hours they spend reading, writing, studying, and even sleeping, and how many hours are spent watching TV or partying. By keeping a schedule, the students see the reality of imbalance on a ledger sheet. This evidence helps because they stop thinking of studying as a "should" activity and more as a balance restorative. A version of this project is valuable for everyone.

In my case, I found my profile radically unlike that of most of my students. My squares for reading, writing, sleeping, and exercising were nicely shaded in. But time allotted for relaxing alone or with friends was minimal. My workaholic nature was plain on the page and was evidence of imbalance.

This exercise can be done as well with personal finances. A priest of the Episcopal cathedral in New York City once told me, "If you want to know what someone is really like, don't listen to their prayers, look at their checkbook." Looking at our checkbook or credit card statement with an eye to identifying different categories of expenditure can be as revealing of our priorities as the schedule sheet for measuring how we spend our time.

We speak of "spending" time. The connection between

spending time and spending money is built into our language. When I look at my latest American Express statement, I see an equal balance of expenditures under restaurants, clothing, books, and CDs, with less spent in the categories of anonymous titillation online and charity, and very little for the downtime of travel. Changing spending patterns based on balance is an Apollonian version of balancing your checkbook.

To be balanced is to be grounded. Leading a balanced life might sound like some bygone classical ideal. But if we translate the virtue into our own jargon we might get at the essence of Apollonian balance. A phrase going around that expresses the meaning of balance or being grounded is "keeping it real." Borrowed from hip-hop culture, "keeping it real" means to make choices that are realistic, or authentic, or practical, rather than those driven by fantasy, posing, fronting, or wishful desire. There is certainly a place for cutaway fantasies and wish fulfillment, no matter how infantile. But what Apollo offers is a principle for making the most important of choices. Apollo isn't just about getting us through the day happily but about getting us through life happily—the two don't always require the same faculty.

Reserve the quality of Apollonian balance, then, for the major issues. If you're deciding who you want to spend the night with, you might want to go crazy and be impetuous. But if someone is offering you his hand as a life partner, you need to ask yourself whether or not you're keeping it real, going for the solid, balanced candidate.

You might want to take a fun job for a while. When I graduated from college, I satisfied a short-lived libidinal fantasy by being a locker room attendant at the Y for a month. But when you're figuring out your next step professionally, you want to keep it real by making a choice based on salary, hours, or personal freedom, rather than how you will be perceived by others. Apollonian balance is admittedly based on pedestrian standard operating procedures. But only advanced gymnasts and yogis, after all, can be as balanced on one foot as on two.

A DATE WITH APOLLO

Devise an Apollonian date. You can either go alone or go with a friend. As Apollo is associated with wisdom and healing through beauty and contemplation, he might lend himself to a solo experience. A god such as Hermes (Chapter Three) is more buddy-buddy and so will be conducive to tandem events or team efforts.

Choosing an Apollonian date is a good opportunity to use your intuition. Just go inside yourself and think of something you'd like to do that makes you feel light, balanced, and good about yourself. All these Greek gods are really different role models. So we're looking here for an activity that makes us feel like Apollo—sunny, absorbed in the beauties of art, music, or poetry. You'll probably find that your gift of intuition will kick in quickly. You'll feel that a certain destination is right. This date is an opportunity to take time to go there.

On my date with Apollo, I opted to visit the Metropolitan Museum of Art. The show I selected was *The Lure of the Exotic: Gauguin in New York Collections.* The Met was an obvious choice. Few locations are more like a Greek temple than the Met, with its high pillars, crescendos of staircases both inside and out, and vast classical main entrance hall filled with light pouring down from above. But a museum was the right choice for uplift for me in a more personal way, too. I was often in a dark funk when I was a kid. Lots of kids are—especially gay kids. I associate a certain amount of disconnectedness and offbeat gloom with my early years.

Yet I could always count on a trip to a local museum in

Scranton, Pennsylvania, to transpose my emotional key from minor to major. If I scanned their collection now in comparison with the Met's, I might not be too impressed. But what I remember as an idiosyncratic gathering of oil paintings, Egyptian artifacts, and geological specimens in long glass cases was then a revelation of a wider world, of civilizations past, and of curators who had selflessly dedicated themselves to the antlike task of bringing these treasures together. I'd leave the museum feeling keyed up and happy. I learned resilience at that museum. Its joys of the spirit helped me to deal with the exigencies of the playground, where I felt much more threatened.

One person's museum is another person's basketball game. My student Frank might get more of an Apollonian shot of light from attending a basketball game. The quality of the afterglow achieved is the proof. In my case, on my Apollonian date I did take in the Gauguin paintings: the colors—tangerine, fuchsia, and rose—on his matte canvases were like a rich mold covering the walls of a lower floor of the Lehman Wing. Given the excuse for this date, I of course visited Apollo, in the form of a chopped marble trunk of a vestige in the lucent hall devoted to ancient Greece and Rome statuary. At lunch in the refectory, I noted scores of white-haired men—the gentlemen who lunch—looking calm and alert as they read the *Times,* presumably taking a break between exhibitions. Above all else they exemplified for me the value of civilization and its contentment. They were showing how the Apollonian spirit could add grace and dignity as punctuation marks to a life intelligently lived.

Making my way back to the Lexington Avenue subway on a humid July afternoon, I felt a familiar zing. This was the curative zing of adolescent afternoons spent in the Scranton museum. During that walk along a town-house–lined street, I thought of the cluster of qualities in each of the Greek gods and of the almost subliminal messages sent by their differing combinations of qualities. I understood, too, Nietzsche's claim that if you just needed one god to fathom the premise of Olympian spirituality, take Apollo. Everything else is fine-tuning. When in doubt, go for the light.

The message I got that day from Apollo—aka the Shining One—was that nothing is wiser than healing. And nothing is more healing than beauty sifted by time or contemplated in the right light.

APOLLONIAN EXERCISES

1. List significant relationships that you've had in your life: trysts, friends, lovers, or partners. Then write down lessons you've learned from these relationships.

2. List friends who elicit a positive feeling and those who elicit a negative feeling. Spend a week with only those on the positive list.

3. Keep track of time spent doing different activities. At the end of a week, draw up a balance sheet of activities. Try to adjust for any imbalances the following week.

Two

DIONYSUS
THE GOD OF SENSUALITY

PROFILE

If Apollo is Mr. Right, Dionysus is the ever-alluring Mr. Wrong. Or Ms. Wrong—for many of Dionysus's qualities come from his sexual ambiguity. A gender bender of a god, he enjoys walking on the wild side, wearing long purple dresses, and encircling his rich mane of curly blond hair in ivy. He was schizophrenically known among the ancient Greeks as *Orthos*, the Erect, and *Enorches*, the Betesticled, while also being nicknamed *Pseudanor*, the Man Without True Virility, *Gynnis*, the Womanish, and *Arsenothelys*, the Man-Womanly. One classical scholar, C. Kerenyi, contrasted him on this score to the most virile of the gods, Zeus: "No other god so much appeared to be a second Zeus as Dionysus did: a Zeus of women."

Ambiguity began at birth for this "twice-born god." Dionysus's mother, Semele, a mortal, was seduced by his father, Zeus, disguised as an ordinary man. But when Semele, clued into her lover's true identity, asked to see him in his godly form, Zeus appeared as a bolt of lightning, and she was instantly toast—her tag becoming Lightning-Married. He saved his unborn son and carried him stitched in his own thigh until giving birth, three months later, to this singular clone of a male born of a male. That Dionysus sprouted horns—like the devil's baby born with amber slits of eyes in *Rosemary's Baby*—is a clue to his affiliation with the dark side, as well as his identification with goats. (Some stories go for the jugular by claiming that Dionysus's mother was Persephone, the queen of the underworld.)

If Apollo's big contribution was lyric music and poetry, Dionysus's was wine. Spreading the love and joys of wine drinking, he spent most of his life on earth wandering through Greece, the Middle East, and India. He was trailed like an androgynous rock star by his fans, mostly women known as bacchantes (from Bacchus, another of his names) or maenads (from their tendency to go into mania, or rages), as well as male *satyrs,* usually pictured with long tails, erect penises, and horns—all of whom raced through the woods accompanied by the sounds of flutes, drums, and tambourines. Along on tour were the *centaurs,* perforated beings who were half man and half horse.

During the 1960s, the poet and classicist Robert Graves tried to prove that these Dionysian rites were not simply a wine tasting, but involved tripping on hallucinogenic mushrooms as well. Graves was intrigued by what he called a "contradictory reputation for wisdom and misdemeanor" among Dionysus's followers, who were rumored to engage in sexual orgies as well as *sparagmos,* the tearing apart and devouring of cows, goats, and sheep. He speculated that "the Maenads' savage custom of tearing off their victims' heads may refer allegorically to tearing off the sacred mushroom's head."

The Greek playwright Euripides devotes one of his more freakish tragedies, *The Bacchae,* to Dionysus and his followers, describing him true to form in the stage directions of the first scene: "Enter Dionysus. He is of soft, even effeminate, appearance. His face is beardless; he is dressed in a fawn-skin and carries a thyrsus (i.e. a stalk of fennel tipped with ivy leaves). On his head he wears a wreath of ivy, and his long blond curls ripple down over his shoulders. Throughout the play he wears a smiling mask" (Arrowsmith translation).

The Bacchae turns on the god's revenge against Pentheus, the ruler of Thebes, "a young man of athletic build," who is trying to snuff out his cult. The pivot of the play occurs when Dionysus tricks this young jock of a king into dressing in drag to go into the woods to observe a Dionysian ritual: "Enter Pentheus from the palace. He wears a long linen dress which partly conceals his fawn-skin. He carries a thyrsus in his hand; on his head he wears a wig with long blond curls bound by a snood. He is dazed and completely in the power of the god who has now possessed him."

Despite or because of his effeminacy and languid eyelashes, Dionysus attracted lots of female lovers, finally marrying Ariadne of Naxos, the daughter of King Minos of Crete. He did have one prominent gay encounter. During a descent to the underworld to rescue his mother after her scorching intercourse with Zeus, Dionysus got lost and asked a guide for directions. The guide was instantly smitten, and said he would help Dionysus only if he would sleep with him. In some versions, this favor is described as a promise of "complete female surrender." Dionysus agreed but insisted on finding his mother first. When he returned to comply with the bargain, the guide had died. In a display of emotion, somewhere between grief, fairness, and bold exhibitionism, he molded a statue to the exact proportions of his own penis and left the glorified dildo at the deceased's tomb.

Dionysus eventually ascended to Mount Olympus to take his rightful place at the right hand of Zeus. As the son of a mortal woman, the youngest son of Zeus, his apotheosis wasn't guaranteed but was earned. He became a god late in life. His eventual transcendence is an important element in the code of Greek mythology. Light and dark, good and bad, wisdom and sexuality are not opposed here. Puritans might well be puzzled by the Greeks' attitude toward kinky Dionysus as a full, holy, and blessed partner in the cosmic scheme. He is identified with intoxication and even madness, but he is also given credit for the social and beneficent powers of wine. Quite positively, he is viewed as the god of civilization, theater, law, and peace.

The Chinese devised the symbol of the yin and yang: a circle divided into light and dark, with a dot of light in the dark half and a dot of dark in the light. Such an emblem of the balance of dark and light forces might well have symbolized the ancient Greeks. It perfectly expresses the rich ambivalence in Olympian spirituality. Dionysus is a bad seed. He drinks too much, experiences bouts of madness, and sleeps around. He's a Mick Jagger type living in a shadow world of groupies. He's the very spirit of the seventies, the golden age of promiscuity. He defies gender. And yet he's a god, a deity. His main contribution to the mix: sheer sensual energy.

MEDITATIONS AND EXERCISES

SENSUALITY AND THE SEVENTIES

I continue to flash on the late seventies and early eighties, especially in New York City and San Francisco, as the epitome of a Dionysian moment. Burned in my brain from that era is *Self-Portrait* (1978) by Robert Mapplethorpe. In this black-and-white photograph, the edgy documenter of so much dark sensuality—dressed only in a black leather vest and chaps—glares back toward the camera with a long tail of a bullwhip sticking out from his ass. A few years later, in *Self-Portrait* (1985), he's simplified the concept: himself, shirtless, with long disheveled hair from which two horns stick up. He's obviously posed as a playful satyr, a follower of Dionysus, from whom our much more damning image of the devil was later drawn.

"Dionysian" and "bacchanalian" were the adjectives overused by journalists to describe many of the unstrung evenings of the seventies—and not just at gay bars or sex clubs such as the Mineshaft. A night at Studio 54 in midtown Manhattan, with its mixed crowd of straights and gays, or at the downtown rock 'n' roll clubs CBGB and the Mudd Club, or at the straight S&M club Chateau 19, always involved revelry, a cocktail of drugs, and the selling of a line of seduction to whoever would or could listen. The lighting was bad, which was good. The escape was elemental and basic. Yet a steep price was paid, even early on, in burnout or disease.

Many of the satyrs of the epoch, the ones who were the models or inspiration for much of Mapplethorpe's notorious work, haunt my memory. One of these dark lights was Gustav von

Will, a German who went by the name Tava, drove a red pickup truck, and made drawings on an abandoned elevated railroad on Manhattan's Lower West Side, above the Eagle's Nest leather bar. Tava, lithe and sensuous, with Dionysian locks, always wore a sleeveless dark-blue denim jacket, on its back side a pattern of tacks spelling out MURDER, INC. beneath the bare outline of a penis. One night he took me up to the railroad to show me the fragile chalk drawings that he'd made every few feet on the pavement, like painted tattoos: a circle of blue stars outlined in shimmering silver; a fiery Tibetan necklace of orange skulls; a cigarette with a gorgeous crimson tip; and a mauve heart painfully pierced by an arrow.

Walking on the wild side continues into the present, of course, with new pharmaceuticals and DJ remixes. A few months—not decades—ago, an article from the metro desk of the *New York Times* began: "Some know it as crystal. Others refer to it as Tina, a campy abbreviation of its other name, Christina. But among the habitués of New York's frenetic gay club scene, the extraordinarily powerful stimulant commonly known as crystal meth is earning a new nickname: the Evil One." The report detailed the rise of methamphetamine, begat from ecstasy, which was begat from cocaine. Both an aphrodisiac and a long-lasting stimulant for dancing, crystal had been adding numbers weekly to the Crystal Meth Anonymous meeting at the gay community center.

The ancient Greeks didn't have methamphetamines. But they did recognize, respect, fear, and celebrate a Dionysian spirit. If you put the Apollonian light together with the Dionysian dark, you have a potent recipe for the high art and culture of ancient Athens. At least, so riffed Nietzsche in *The*

Birth of Tragedy, where he compared the tension between these two tendencies as "perpetual strife" until "eventually, by a metaphysical miracle of the Hellenic 'will,' they appear coupled with each other, and through this coupling ultimately generate an equally Dionysian and Apollonian form of art—Attic tragedy."

The development of the tragedies of ancient Greece—Sophocles' *Oedipus Tyrannus* or Euripides' *Medea*—is a good case study of how a balance of light and dark can be achieved. Even if the story of their development is simplified by Nietzsche for argument's sake and many historical details lost, the bottom line seems clear: tragedy evolved out of Dionysian rites. What is evoked in them is the memory of earlier happenings, where people would sing, dance, or whirl, achieving some sort of trance, perhaps with the help of wine and hallucinogens, perhaps with the help of sexual activity. The modern analogy would be the disco or, with the drug ecstasy, the rave.

From this communal beat, so the story goes, developed the more controlled theater of Dionysus, located in the temple of Dionysus in the middle of Athens, where the Great Dionysia festival was held each spring. What might have begun as a mosh pit of song and dance was now a spectator sport, with all Athenians welcome to sit in the rows of seats carved in semicircles in the side of a hill. Instead of risking madness or death, the audience could experience a healing release by safely watching masked actors portray mythological beings caught up short by their own excesses or crashing into an implacable fate. In Nietzsche's terms, an Apollonian light had been shed on the goings-on.

Experimenting with the Dionysian can yield a positive return, but only if the blinking yellow caution light implicit in the myth is heeded—for madness or the threat of madness always shadows Dionysus. Hera, jealous that her husband, Zeus, had conceived him with another woman, first drove young Dionysus mad when she tracked him down in Syria. Apollo must be the guiding principle. Healing and common sense must always come first and must be the beginning and end of any circle of self-knowledge. But the gods and heroes who cross over to the dark side or descend into the underworld, Dionysus included, always return stronger, wiser, and often kinder. Certainly Mapplethorpe and Tava, among others, were paradoxically among the gentlest and most sensual men I've ever met. As the fierce, effeminate god describes himself in *The Bacchae:*

> *Dionysus, son of Zeus, consummate god,*
> *most terrible, and yet most gentle, to mankind.*
> (ARROWSMITH TRANSLATION)

BAD-BOY SENSUALITY

I've recently taken up bicycling. My machine: a ten-speed, gray-green Trek Hybrid mountain bike.

Biking has added another dating option to my life. Indeed, it's rapidly becoming the dating activity of first choice, not solely because of the advantage of aerobic exercise, but also because of the hidden advantage of having a meaningful dialogue. Aristotle's school of philosophy was described as Peripatetic because he would teach while walking through his academy, the Lyceum. Socrates in Plato's dialogues was often portrayed as walking while chatting his way through a philosophical argument. Perhaps cycling is just a higher-tech version, a combine of thought, motion, and oxygen to the brain.

One of my favorite bicycling partners is Dean, a tall New Orleans native in his late thirties, with cropped black hair and long sideburns, who I met at the gym a few months back. In appearance, he always reminds me of a Confederate soldier or Rhett Butler: a likable villain. In practice, he's a counselor for disturbed adolescents, a social worker, and actually that rarest of animals, a good guy.

Late one Saturday afternoon we were taking a sunset spin around Central Park. Dean would catch up to me, or I to him, and we'd exchange a few words or phrases between breaths. Then a hill would present itself, and I'd become absorbed in the miracle of shifting gears, navigating the steep hill as easily as if I were pedaling on a flat boardwalk, leaving behind a trail of pale, exhausted runners with sweat running off their bodies.

As we zoomed onto a less rugged road skirting the manicured south end of the park, before jamming into the rush of traffic to Lincoln Center curtain time, I tried out some of my latest Dionysian notions of experimentation on Dean.

"So that means you're gonna get wrecked on whiskey and wine all the time?" he asked.

"No, no," I said, worrying through the issue myself. I'd sailed through many latitudes of intoxication and no longer had the constitution.

"But that's what 'Dionysian' means," he complained, obviously getting annoyed, more annoyed than the conversation merited.

"No. It's a state of mind."

"But why bother? What's the point?"

Both of us instinctively pulled over to the curb for a resolution.

"Dean, if you hadn't been a pothead, and hadn't gone to re-hab, you wouldn't be the person you are today. You wouldn't be as good a counselor. Admit it."

"Mmm, maybe you're right."

Point taken, we wheeled off toward the stone-and-metal scrim of buildings that rises like a wall at Central Park South, rendered fantastic and fiery when the sun sets on a clear day from the correct tangent.

We then sliced through the glister and continued down Avenue of the Americas.

I'd arrived at an important personal distinction during that outing. Whatever the cultural necessity of the 1970s, the moment for a Great Dionysia had passed: been there, done that. The conclusion that "sex, drugs, and rock 'n' roll" was a literal prescription for integration seemed thin as well. Finally, these were as much metaphors as recipes for specific cocktails.

Even the character Dionysus in Euripides' *The Bacchae* disputes the popular association of his cult with sexual orgies. His was no Hellfire Club, he argues. Indeed, though the denouement of the tragedy is King Pentheus's crazed mother sleepwalking onstage, flourishing the decapitated head of her son on a stick, the tabloid version of what went on in those hills at night is a record set straight by the playwright. He has the prophet Tiresias testify as a character witness to the chastity of Dionysus's followers:

Always and in every case
it is her character and nature that keeps

a woman chaste. But even in the rites of Dionysus,
the chaste woman will not be corrupted.

(ARROWSMITH TRANSLATION)

In the same play, Tiresias talks of wine, not only as a lubricant for ferocious behavior but as possessing a kinder, gentler aspect as well:

> *For filled with that good gift,*
> *suffering mankind forgets its grief; from it*
> *comes sleep; with it oblivion of the troubles*
> *of the day. There is no other medicine*
> *for misery.*

Because of this mollifying influence of wine, Dionysus was also known by the most positive of titles, Savior and Deliverer.

Folded into the divine traits of the gods is always a quality that touches human life more personally. Apollo is the god of wisdom, but the quality of his that touches our lives is healing. Dionysus is the god of sensuality, yet immersion in the Dionysian element causes, as well, a relaxing of the habit of judging, and the result may be forgiveness, tolerance, compassion, and pity.

King Pentheus in *The Bacchae* is presented as an intolerant boor. In the language of the bohemian beat poets, he'd be a square. An ancient Greek word close in meaning was *amathes*. Pentheus is described as a man of *amathia* because he's judgmental, harsh, inflexible, and lacking in self-knowledge. He's the bully who's trying to pick on Dionysus. In another play by

Euripides, *Electra*, Orestes states that pity (*to oiktos*) is never found among the *amatheis* but only among the wise (*sophoi*). He says, "We who are educated pity much." By "educated" he means those who are able to find their way around their inner selves.

A favorite tool of some transactional psychotherapists has been the "little kid"—the notion of our having internalized different family roles as part of our adult selves. If an anxious patient is feeling more tightly wound than usual, or overly ornery, or downright angry and reciting a long list of grievances, a prod from a transactional therapist might be: "The little kid is acting up. What can you do for the little kid?" That reminder can become a sort of "Open sesame!" I learned long ago that if I'm being tough on others, angry at their shortcomings, I'm probably denying myself a double dip of sensual pleasure. The longer the denial, the more pressure builds up into the inevitable pop of the magnum of relaxation. And with relaxation come joy, peace, and often tolerance.

In Euripides' play, Pentheus doesn't really want to stomp out all those Dionysian pleasure romps. If he were a little bit wiser, he'd know that what he really wants to do is dress up in a shift, put on a blond wig, go out in the woods, and play with super-sized dildos with the rest of the satyrs. He'd probably return to the palace in central-city Thebes feeling a lot kinder and gentler toward himself and others.

DIONYSIAN EXERCISE #1

Wait until you're feeling pent-up, frustrated, or angry, then indulge in some bad behavior. Leaving drugs and alco-

hol off the list, find activities that trigger your sense of indulging the delinquent malcontent within.

My list of innocuous-enough bad behavior has included

- Revisiting my collection of vintage *Drummer* porn magazines
- Smoking cigarettes and drinking *Jolt,* a high-octane caffeine drink
- Channel surfing for hours
- Calling my partner in crime, Luis, to go cruising for trouble
- Skulking around XXX websites in the middle of the afternoon

The trademark Dionysian gesture is to pour a glass of wine, which is fine if you don't suffer from alcoholism. But the point of this exercise is to discover personal gestures that have the same relaxing effect—wine equivalents. The more wine equivalents you can bring up from your psychic cellar, the more chance you have of avoiding becoming too tightly wound.

Some of the activities on my own list are perfectly healthy: Luis and I are more talk than action. But other items are not so benign. Apollo would never smoke cigarettes or drink Jolt. Nor would he allow himself to be lulled by TV or raunchy porn. These are definite sedatives. If used to excess, they might result in brain death, and of course, there is no excuse for that. But the beauty of the ancient Greek system of checks and balances is that there is a place for them in achieving wisdom. You just have to read the warning label on the bottle first.

SENSUAL CROSS-DRESSING

Although Dionysus has fewer love affairs with men to his name than Apollo, he's the god most likely to be labeled bisexual. Like Marilyn Manson or other glam or goth types, though, his bisexuality is mostly aesthetic. Giving a G-rated explanation of this behavior, C. Kerenyi wrote of some of the nicknames of Dionysus:

> The surname Dyalos, "the hybrid," must certainly refer to a hermaphroditic being, and together with the other names of the sort must be derived from hushed-up tales of the god's bisexuality. But such surnames as Dendrus, Dendrites, Endendros, "the tree god" or "he in the tree," or the names connected with vegetable luxuriance and growth, such as Phelon, Phleus, or Phloios, indicate that what is meant is not a human sexual hybridity, but the bisexuality that is characteristic of most trees and constitutes their natural completeness.

Whether you're a tree or a god, bisexuality adds extra options to the menu. My cycling buddy Dean began going out with a woman a few years ago. He felt exhausted by the crazy dating patterns among gays. His circuit breaker had been tripped. But when he told his mother of his new girlfriend she warned: "You can be gay or you can be straight, but you can't be both. Bisexuals are just greedy." Dionysus was certainly greedy, as were most of the Greek gods. But finally his bisexuality was as much a pose as a way of life. Or rather, posing was a big part of his sexuality. He was the god most into vogueing.

Dionysus was even more about cross-dressing than about

swinging. If Apollo's favorite item of clothing was the laurel wreath, symbolizing wisdom and poetry, Dionysus's was the ivy wreath, symbolizing partying. His mode was more playful than proactive; his contribution to the pantheon was his playful ego-bending behavior. Bending the rules has produced some leaps in human progress: the list of inventors or entrepreneurs who dropped out of school, for instance, is not short. Coloring outside the box is a prescription for success in business. But no rules are more resistant to being bent than those we've made up for ourselves. Dionysus offers the sort of benefit that comes from coloring outside the box of our own personality.

Camille O'Grady was a club torch singer who worked a punk look in the seventies. She was an honorary member of the Mineshaft, where she would hang in male drag. One of her underground lyrics that caught on among her devoted fans expressed a very Dionysian sentiment: "The mind is a dress. Change it!" Stepping out in psychic—or actual—drag is an important phase in the procurement of Dionysian self-knowledge.

DIONYSIAN EXERCISE #2

Dress, behave, or think in a way that runs counter to your usual mode. Try this off-dressing experiment every day for a week, or put on one "new dress" for the entire week.

Among the uncharacteristic new looks or moves I tried out:

- Greased-back hair
- Wearing a slew of colored handkerchiefs in my back pocket at a leather bar

- Working out in black Lycra shorts with yellow side stripes
- Taking a new route to habitual destinations: bookstore, Urban Outfitters, Dean's apartment
- Dancing until six in the morning
- Calling three people I find sexy and who I've never called or haven't called in a while

The simplest way to experience a Dionysian release is to dress counterclockwise from your usual mode. Grease in the hair seemed to say, "I care about how I look"—a message I avoid. The Lycra shorts in the gym were an affectation I felt reserved for a kind of gym rat—younger, more muscular, and more likely to read *HX*, a trendy gay magazine. I never did colored handkerchiefs—because they signified to me "macho daddy" in the complex semiotics of leather bars. Seeming out of character, all these departures in style took my breath away a bit. But I admit I didn't notice much change in response from others—a lesson in itself. We are often attached to our notion of ourselves in a magnified fashion. Such off-dressing puts personality in proportion.

Changes in behavior may feel more substantial. During my Dionysian phase, I went dancing with a friend at an aptly named club, Amnesia (Anesthesia might have been an even more apt name), while on a summer vacation on Ibiza. I was amazed at my dumb joy when the dry ice machine blew a cool pink breeze in my face, and even more amazed when I walked out at six in the morning. "Dancing is great exercise," I blurted out, a bit late in the game, having not been dancing in at least three years.

Thinking of and then contacting three sexy people you

wouldn't normally have called can be a good exercise in integration. Part of the significance of Dionysus in Greek mythology is that sexual energy is divine, too. The goal in this experiment is not so much doing the deed as, rather, taking impulses from our Dionysian dynamo as seriously as those from the brain (for professional networking) or heart (for pure affection, friendship, or love). Because sexuality is not rational or always moral, we may tuck its impulses away. Making those calls can feel like a dare. I'm not guaranteeing a call back. But if you try this exercise—and like me have tended to be overly laid-back or cool in this regard—you'll probably find that energy can be its own reward.

A DATE WITH DIONYSUS

The only way to have a successful date with Dionysus is to give in to the fun. He's very much a "show me the way to the next whiskey bar" type deity who just won't stop.

Dating Dionysus is impulse dating. The first move on a date with Dionysus is locating the dark clutch in the stomach that gets your heart racing. The challenge here is to let Dionysus whisper his dirty words in your ear without going for the obvious—getting smashed or high.

I knew immediately where to go for my Dionysian date: Pork Night at the Lure. The Lure is a classic leather bar in the meatpacking district of Lower Manhattan. Pork is a Wednesday-night-only event. It bills itself as "one of the cleverest and most artistic nights in New York," with a pig for a logo and "Squeal!" as its advertising slogan. Here the usual leather motif is updated by East Village types in Doc Martens with pert goatees rather than traditional seventies scruffy mustaches or beards. The music is hard-driving industrial rock: Joy Division, Black Flag. The space, with its trademark pool table and porn video monitors, is overlaid with candles, factory detritus, devil masks, and canvases painted with lurid color by young artists.

As with most dates, getting there is half the thrill. Not used to being out of my apartment after my self-imposed curfew on a school night, I found the walk through Greenwich Village on a steamy summer's night a pleasant descent into a Dionysian mood. The moon was a lemon yellow wafer. The cobblestone streets magnified footsteps in evocative echoes. On the hunt, so many passersby seemed to be looking for something. Of course, this is a particularly urban phenomenon. But I've been to such bars in other parts of the country, where the drive is invariably to an out-of-the-way shopping center or warehouse district on the furtive edges of town.

Dionysus was being featured at Pork Night in more ways than I'd expected. But now, of course, my eyes were trained for clues. Lots of those scuffing around were mimicking a satyr look. They were self-conscious beasts with long hair, long side-burns, and exposed hairy chests. Dionysus was hardly porcine, but subhuman metamorphosis was evident in the goat imper-sonations of his satyrs. To embolden me in feeling that I wasn't entirely imagining this mythology come to life, a smooth-skinned Latino artist, dressed only in jockstrap and pink flip-flops, perched on a high platform, was painting a ten-foot-high satyr with horns, scratchy goatee, humongous penis, and a prong of a tail, on a vast paper canvas. His smaller encrusted oil paintings stacked nearby were of demonic purple faces from which licked bright orange tongues.

The main event at Pork is a performance, which can be a whipping, a candle dripping, or someone slicing his own arm with a razor. By midnight, the performing hour, the bar was full. ("Don't any of these people have jobs?" is a common thought balloon indicating that you're in a Dionysian spot.) The perfor-mance that night was a weird penitential ritual. A small Asian dominatrix with an ivory face, costumed in a nun's habit, stuck acupuncture needles into the forehead and through the skin, chest, and back, of a nubile guy with a long, Saint John of the Cross face, tied to a wooden beam. Her crucified victim, dressed only in a loincloth and boots, had the walleyed expression of a transfixed deer. The tone of the presentation wobbled between horror and kitsch.

"This is why I never leave my apartment," said my dentist, who happened to be standing next to me.

Set up in a booth in the back hallway was a tarot card reader who charged me ten bucks to look into his pack full of mystical symbols—candles burning, staves crossed, a man hanging upside down. He told me that I was "hazy": "You have good energy. You're in a good place in the universe. But you're a little stuck right now. If a change came along, you'd welcome it." He scowled, though, when I expressed disagreement with his findings.

Arriving at Pork at 11 P.M., I'd slipped my Swiss army watch into my jeans pocket. The plan: spend an hour, with twenty minutes to get home, so I would still be asleep at a regular hour. But soon enough it was 2 A.M. I'd become hypnotized by the slow-motion circulation of quite a few "hazy" men. Some of those circling stopped to talk:

"I'm here looking for a top. I have two bottoms at home."

"Are you a casting agent or something?" I asked jokingly.

"I used to be. How'd you know? What's the problem in New York? Is it ninety percent bottom? Ten percent top?"

I eventually drank two bottles of Pure Pride water and smoked two cigarettes. Years ago I'd practically needed to be electrocuted to feel jolted on a night out. Now two cigarettes seemed to be enough of a price paid for transport to the underworld.

By 3 A.M. I was in bed. By noon I was up. My next day was thrown off. A pleasant, sensuous disinterest set in instead, a virtual hangover. The phone call I'd been stressed to make yesterday seemed unimportant. The magazine piece I'd been intent to pitch faded. Instead I was experiencing a woozy gladness. Such oblivion is the true trademark of a date with Dionysus— causing forgetfulness and distraction from pain, restoring peace and a feeling of communion with all the other horned beasts.

The chorus of women followers chants this sentiment in rhythmic poetry in their hymn to Dionysus in Euripides' *The Bacchae:*

> *In various ways one man outraces another in the*
> *race for wealth and power.*
> *Ten thousand men possess ten thousand hopes.*
> *A few bear fruit in happiness; the others go awry.*
> *But he who garners day by day the good of life,*
> *he is happiest. Blessed is he.*

(ARROWSMITH TRANSLATION)

DIONYSIAN EXERCISES

1. Wait until you're feeling pent-up, frustrated, or angry. Then indulge in some bad behavior. Leaving drugs and alcohol off the list, find activities that trigger your own sense of expressing the delinquent malcontent within.

2. Dress, behave, or think in a way that runs counter to your usual mode. Try this off-dressing experiment every day for a week, or put on one "new dress" for the entire week.

Three

HERMES
THE GOD OF COMMUNICATION

PROFILE

Hermes was basically the bike messenger of the gods, without the bike. You could see him coming at the speed of light from 186,300 miles per second away. As the divine messenger, he was outfitted in distinctive drag. Equipped with gold wings on his sandals, he was as deft as any UPS delivery guy. He wore a round helmet to protect him from the rain and carried the *kerykeion* (or *caduceus*, in Latin), a winged staff entwined with two copulating snakes, since swiped by doctors, postal workers, and diplomats for their own insignia. Sometimes pictured as a bearded middle-aged man, he grew younger and younger as fashions changed, until he was finally *Teen People* material, his bare torso sinewy and smooth.

The son of the nymph Maia and Zeus, who apparently frequented quite a few nymphs' grottoes, Hermes is the god of communication in most of its forms: speech, the Greek alphabet, and the musical scale. The adjective taken from his name, "hermeneutic," is applied to interpretation done by literary scholars on texts. Like all the gods and goddesses, though, Hermes is not simply a good guy—he is also a thief and a liar. His mastery of the arts of communication, like Dionysus's of wine, could be applied to either positive or negative ends. When he was one day old, he had already stolen Apollo's herd of cattle, driven them backward to confuse any trackers, slaughtered two, and then crept back into his cradle, where he wrapped himself cleverly in his Baby Gap swaddling.

If there had been a need for a god of either capitalism or fashion, Hermes would have been booked. He was indeed the god of commerce. When Apollo tried to pin him with cattle robbery, he wound up being bought off by Hermes' new lyre, which he had constructed from a tortoise shell and cow gut. The stock exchange might well be a temple of Hermes, and insider trading a classic Hermeneutic activity. He was the broker for Zeus's delicate negotiations, including stealing away the Trojan prince Ganymede for a lover. The constant shuttling of the world of fashion, with looks borrowed from music videos showing up on the runways of New York and Milan, is very him.

In the virtual body of the pantheon, Hermes' body part is the leg. He is the god of all forms of travel. The other body part that keeps popping up in his iconography is the phallus. Dating back perhaps to some bygone anthropological era when flashing privates established a territorial imperative, the herm, or phallic statue—originally stones piled atop one another—was a common property marker in ancient Greece. Hermes, the wayfarer, forever crossing boundaries in his travels, including down to the underworld as the god of graves and up through the night sky as god of astronomy, was honored with these stone dildos. They were considered sacred.

Hermes had no wives, but he did have many sons, at least three of whom were anatomically gifted. The first, Hermaphroditus, the son and/or daughter of Hermes and Aphrodite, was born with both female breasts and male genitals. His second son, Pan, was one of the phallic gods, as was another rumored son, the well-endowed Priapus. This emphasis on legs and penises advertises as well Hermes' godly oversight of the gym and athletes; he invented boxing and gymnastics. Locker room talk would qualify as a classic Hermeneutic ritual. As the historian Walter Burkert wrote in *Greek Religion* of the most famous statue of Hermes, by Praxitiles, in Olympia: "In this shape Hermes becomes, along with Eros and Heracles, the god of athletic youth . . . and gymnasia; here the phallic, homoerotically tinged element is still very much in evidence."

In life as in literature, Hermes is the god responsible for keeping the plot moving. In the *Iliad,* when the gods want King Priam of Troy to meet with Achilles about the retrieval of his son Hector's corpse, Hermes appears to Priam disguised as a youth, "with beard new grown, which is the most graceful time of young manhood." He takes over the reins of the king's chariot, casts sleep on the Achaean sentries, opens the gate to the courtyard of Achilles' tent, and finally vanishes, after briefly introducing himself:

"Aged sir, I who came to you am a god immortal,
Hermes. My father sent me down to guide and go with you.
But now I am going back again, and I will not go in

Before the eyes of Achilleus, for it would make others angry
For an immortal god so to face mortal men with favour."

(LATTIMORE TRANSLATION)

Hermes' messages are not poetic outpourings of soul, like Apollo's, or trance lyrics, like Dionysus's. Rather, they are practical forms of communication: exercise instructions, restaurant guides, office memos, or phone numbers scratched on the back of a bank statement. Hermes is the interactive god, the god of community. His messages arrive in a polyglot of languages. Like him, the ink in which his messages are written in the events of daily life is often invisible. But his messages are worth learning how to decipher, as the Homeric epithet of Hermes was Luck-Bringing Messenger.

MEDITATIONS AND EXERCISES

GYMS AND COMMUNICATION

When President John F. Kennedy announced a national physical fitness program in the early 1960s, the possibility of an amateur athletics boom on the scale we have seen in the last quarter century seemed remote. At the time of his initiative, adults rarely wore sneakers, and kids mostly wore one brand: black or white high-top Converse All Stars with rubber circles on the ankles. In the past few decades, a clear sign of the sports trend has been the proliferation of sneaker boutiques entirely devoted to the dissemination of new brands and models—Reebok, New Balance, Adidas, Vans, Nike, and Puma.

Likewise, a half century ago, the YMCA was often the only gym available in small towns and many cities. Its usual decor consisted of dank changing rooms, rusting lockers, and cold, overly chlorinated Olympic-sized swimming pools. I remember, in my own small-town Y in northeastern Pennsylvania, boys and men taking showers in the moldy wet room and then wrapping themselves in threadbare white towels. I don't remember any free weights, and certainly no Nautilus machines. In its close affiliate, my high school gymnasium, boys would run laps and perform calisthenics holding army rifles as extra weights. We spent much time throwing around a bitterly named brown medicine ball.

Again, sophisticated choice has set in. Not only are there now gyms, in the plural, but there are niche gyms. Every neighborhood has its own. Every income bracket has its own. Every personality type has its own (including, still, the Y for a retro experience). Although suburban areas might have less density, the choice remains wide. A general move has occurred beyond a single option to offerings such as the Gold's franchises for iron men and serious triathletes, and family-friendly community recreation centers with too many Ping-Pong tables.

Not since ancient Greece has the gym been such a nexus for sending and receiving messages, for crossing borders, and for growing in body as well as in self-knowledge. There's more to gyms, after all, than rock-climbing walls. Developed over centuries of trial and experience, the wisdom of ancient Greek mythology is evident in its embodying the god of the gymnasium and the god of communication in a single, hybrid deity. Hermes gets around. He's always moving. So, naturally, he's the god of movement, involved in gymnastics and wrestling. But the more you move, the more other moving bodies you encounter. Hermes sets the tone for the overlap of all frequencies of communication, from invisible thoughts or spoken comments to the arm around a sculpted shoulder.

The gymnasium for the ancient Greeks generated lots of opportunities for philosophy, as well as for lots of seductive heat. The locale comes up often in the philosophical dialogues of Plato, which were mostly set in Athens during the fifth century B.C. As K. J. Dover laid out the scene in his *Greek Homosexuality:* "The gymnasium as a whole or the wrestling-school (*palaistra*) in particular provided opportunities for looking at naked boys, bringing oneself discreetly to a boy's notice in the hope of eventually speaking to him (for the gymnasium functioned as a social centre for males who could afford leisure), and even touching a boy in a suggestive way, as if by accident, while wrestling with him."

In Aristophanes' *The Birds,* a hit comedy in ancient Athens, a character imagines a chance meeting with a handsome boy, "all rosy from his bath and exercise," as the perfect occasion for making a move. Alcibiades, a young general, recounts in Plato's *Symposium* the role-reversal of his trying to seduce his older hero, Socrates, in the obvious setting, the gym: "After that I invited him to come to the gymnasium with me and we exercised together; I thought I would get somewhere that way. So we exercised together and wrestled on many occasions with no one around—and what can I tell you? I got nowhere" (Christopher Gill translation).

Obviously, the Greek gyms weren't named Crunch or Equinox. One of the more popular was Mikkos, named after its founder, like Radu's Physical Culture Studio, the David Barton Gym, or even the Body by Jake home gym. But the dynamics were entirely familiar. In the establishing scene of Plato's early dialogue *Charmides*, Socrates—the usual protagonist, whose words and actions Plato claimed only to have been recording—plays head games, this time in the lobby of what sounds like a traditionally cruisy gym, Taureas's wrestling school, south of the Acropolis. Having been away in Potidae, Socrates inquires of his friend Critias about "what was happening in the field of philosophy; had any of the young men become pre-eminent for wisdom or beauty or both?" (Donald Watt translation)

Critias's vote was for Charmides. In this dialogue, devoted to proving the axiom "Health of body is dependent on health of soul," the following exchange takes place as the men stare at Charmides, whom Socrates finds "amazingly tall and handsome":

Chaerephon called to me and said, "What do you think of our young man, Socrates? Hasn't he got a lovely face?"

"Extraordinarily lovely," I replied.

"But just let him be persuaded to strip and you won't notice he's got a face at all, his body is so perfectly beautiful."

Well, the others said the same as Chaerephon, and I said, "Goodness, how irresistible you make him sound, provided that he happens to have just one other little thing."

"What's that?" asked Critias.

"Provided that he happens to be endowed with a fine soul," I said.

(DONALD WATT TRANSLATION)

For Socrates, the gymnasium, social life, and discourse were important components of the search for truth. The dialogue *Charmides,* named for the famously beautiful and athletic young man (if Plato were alive today, would there be a dialogue named *Brad Pitt?*), uses discursive logic to prove the holistic relation of physical and spiritual beauty. But it's also proved by the setup itself. Socrates is stimulated in his thinking by the excitement of beautiful bodies, and also by the excitement of the collision of personalities and ideas in the human pinball machine of the gym.

Likewise, gyms are ideal locales for us in the pursuit of self-knowledge. To know which muscles in your spiritual body might need exercise, fear is actually a helpful indicator. As fat is to the body, so fear can be to the soul—evidence of neglect, imbalance, or dysfunction. One of the roles of Hermes is *psychopompos,* or "soul leader," as he guides the souls of the dead with his shepherd's crook down to Hades, the final frontier. For this function, he was a favorite deity of twentieth-century psychologists, such as Carl Jung, for whom he became a symbol of navigating through the dark night of the soul. He was the role model for guiding souls through the personal demons and monsters uncovered in psychoanalysis.

Hermes accelerated in his progress as a tour guide by facing down his fears. While fear might seem an exaggerated concern in such a light context as a gym, nevertheless most boundaries are set up by us, for ourselves, internally, and are demarcated by a slight line of fear or insecurity. The gym is a good place for confronting and crossing physical, personal, and social boundaries. If the fear were anything more than slight, we'd be agoraphobic (from the Greek *agora*, "marketplace"), and we would be afraid to go outside our homes and mingle in the public square, where Socrates did much of his philosophizing.

As exercise routines progress, increasing in difficulty and duration, so exercises using the gym as an agora for health and wisdom can be stepped up. Everyone has a different capacity, history, and starting point. The activities transpiring in a gym constitute a broadband of choices for beginner, intermediate, and advanced.

HERMENEUTIC EXERCISE #1

Create new workouts for yourself, including physical, personal, and social challenges.

My workout program included

- Following the *Navy SEAL Workout*
- Taking a stretch class
- Trying out a different gym

If you haven't done much exercise at all, then simply buying a book or tape or following a TV exercise show to do some basic exercises is progress. I purchased the *Navy SEAL Workout* to be less dependent on my trainer for my every strengthening move. I took the stretch class because, like some awkward high school student at a dance, I'd always felt a bit shy when I'd seen the Busby Berkeley–style circle of guys at the gym doing sideways bends in front of the mirror. Reliving my own teen angst, I slightly feared teams, and here was a team, and a few new team players to meet as well. My visit to Crunch for the first time gave me an opening-day-of-school rush.

POSSES AND COMMUNICATION

Most books in the category the *New York Times Book Review* labels "Advice, How-To and Miscellaneous" use a heterosexual paradigm. Even gay-friendly authors tend to draw all their examples and illustrations from straight life, family, and community. One of the few books to break from this tacit approach in the past few years has been *The Power of Now* by Eckhart Tolle, a German author living in Vancouver. Subtitled *A Guide to Spiritual Enlightenment,* the book caught on through the least cynical of low-tech marketing devices, reader buzz. In one or two pages, Tolle addresses the homosexual paradigm and the singularity of the gay spiritual profile. In the Q&A format of the book, the question he poses for himself is, "In the quest for enlightenment, is being gay a help or a hindrance, or does it not make any difference?" His answer, wisely enough, is mixed.

On the "help" side, Tolle argues that uncertainty about sexual orientation among gays often leads them outside the paradigm of the world handed to them by their parents, teachers, friends, and the media. This sense of being different, while painful, leads to a heightened awareness of ways in which so many "normal" people seem to be living on automatic pilot. On the "hindrance" side, Tolle warns of the danger—at least as far as absolute enlightenment is concerned—in overidentification with "gay" as the final answer to all the questions brought up during the more angst-driven phase of coming out. His misgiving is that "gay" can become a shared identity, an agreed-upon mask, or a series of status symbols (body, boyfriend, and beach house) that wind up trapping people all over again. "You will play roles and games dictated by a mental image you have of yourself as gay," he writes.

Not only in ego formation and cultivation of a higher consciousness, but also in finding partners, lovers, friends, and a community, gays have been given the utopian assignment in recent decades of sketching solutions to social life on a mostly blank page. When the disco smoke cleared, a need to hook up in more ways than the sexual and erotic remained. A timely essay by Edmund White that ran in *Christopher Street* magazine in the early eighties claimed that among many gay men, "friendship . . . has taken the place of love. Sex is casual, romance short-lived; the real continuity in many people's lives comes from their friends." This approach was balanced, of course, in the nineties by a crusade for gay marriage and gay adoption, and for the fiscal and legal advantages of such legal commitments.

Finding a boyfriend is important and challenging, but so is getting a life. One of the configurations I've clocked among a group of my friends is the posse—a multiplied version of White's friendship. They go to bars, restaurants, and parties as a group, and they sometimes even sit together in front of a flat-screen TV displaying a simulated log burning in a fireplace. They share a kind of five-way intimacy. When I went with my favorite posse to a Tuesday-nights-only gay night, called Beige, at the Bowery Bar on Manhattan's Lower East Side, I was impressed by their only-in-gay-America social mix: a TV commercial producer from Los Angeles; a Dominican Banana Republic sales clerk; a fashion photographer; a painter; a Russian bodybuilder in search of a green card; an Israeli shoe salesman who moonlights as a doorman at a dance club. Every night they fold a few extras into their cast.

As in a nineteenth-century novel of manners—Jane Austen's *Emma* or *Pride and Prejudice*—social constraints were palpable. There was more going on at the table with its flickering white votive candles than strip steaks medium-rare. Among the unspoken questions vibrating at the edges of their chat: Would the producer leave with the bodybuilder? Would the Israeli be jealous? Would the Russian's best friend reveal that he had already met me on an AOL coffee date? Why wasn't the Israeli introducing the *Vanity Fair* celebrity reporter, who stopped by the table, to the Dominican, though he'd introduced him to the rest of us? When the evening ended, no one went home with anyone.

Here was a complex social etiquette, but the evening's solution was civilized and apparently deemed by its members to be well worth its discontents. I asked my friend the photographer how the posse came to behave in that way. "Well, it's a trade-off," he explained. "It seems crazy not to be able to pick up Vlad because Bill might be offended. But then, when you go home with strangers, there's always the next morning. It all evaporates. At least with our friends we know they'll be there the next day." They have replaced relationship, in the singular, with community, in the plural.

The posse isn't the only available alternative to the model of the mom-and-pop couple. A woman friend recently noted of gay families she encountered on a subway after a pride march, "There didn't seem to be any generation gap. Both parents and kids had tattoos and piercings. They dressed alike and all seemed quite happy, like friends." When I was at the gay Cathedral of Hope in Dallas, Texas, which is a church belonging to the gay denomination the Metropolitan Community Church (M.C.C.), I observed how much like posses were the many intentional gay families filling the congregation, created by adoption, artificial insemination, or divorce.

HERMENEUTIC EXERCISE #2

Identify your own posse by making a list or drawing a map. See how many different kinds of close relationships you have, and how—or if—they overlap and intersect.

While I have no central figure in my relationship map, I do have lots of players. Indeed, what I found from doing this exercise was five different circles of posses that overlapped, so that a member of one posse might often just as well be a member of another. My drawing looked more like a country hoedown made of simultaneously revolving circles than a romantic slow dance. All that was missing was a hillbilly announcer shouting, "Change your partner and do-si-do."

When I was in my early twenties, I had a vivid daydream. Lying on my bed in the middle of the afternoon, I pictured a blurry guy sitting down and talking to me about how the friendships and connections you make in life were what it's all about. I envisioned as well a map lit up like an electronic Civil War battlefield map with all of these personal connections. If I were an archaic Greek, I might have interpreted the daydream as a visit from Hermes. Its message: I didn't have enough friends, and the ones I had, I kept isolated and apart from one another in discreet, separate boxes. That situation has definitely changed.

SYNCHRONICITY: COMMUNICATING WITH THE UNIVERSE

Hermes invented the game of knucklebones, a kind of divinatory dice. He was poaching, as usual, on Apollo's territory, his tampering with the future veering dangerously close to the job description of the oracle of Delphi. But Hermes' intention was different. His casting of the dice was serious fun rather than actual weather reporting, his skill at the Olympian gaming tables emphasizing his character as the divine trickster, a figure of ever-changing colors, as aleatory as a crapshoot. For example, a chance windfall, like finding a twenty-dollar bill, would have been generally described as a *hermaion* in ancient Greek.

Hermes' divinatory dice were similar to runes, which have enjoyed a recent revival. Cut into short sticks or engraved on smooth flat pebbles, runes were an alphabet created by the ancient German and Norse peoples. They were a kind of alphabet made of symbols of human and animal forms, parts of the human body, weapons, swastikas, suns, wheels, swirls, squares, and circles, which gradually took on sacred meanings as the first true oracle of the pagan tribes of northern Europe. The Roman historian Tacitus, in his first-century chronicle *Germania,* gave an account of watching the casting of these runes: "They cut a branch from a fruit bearing tree and divided it into small pieces; these they mark with certain distinctive signs and scatter them at random and without order upon a white cloth."

Experimenting with a modern manufactured collection of runes on a Sunday afternoon, I reached into the green velvet bag from the kit I'd bought, with a defined intention—as suggested by the instructions—for guidance on a particular subject: the writing of this book. I received a remarkably Hermes-friendly rune, an awkward *R* that signified, in its traditional meaning: "a journey, riding, carriage; refers to the soul after death." I wasn't at all spooked by the death reference, opting to stress to myself the coincidence of Hermes as the god both of travel and of guiding souls after death. In the companion volume, *The Healing Runes,* my rune was interpreted by the modern authors as signifying "surrender": "Drawing this Rune is an invitation to turn your will and your life over to God."

Carl Jung was fascinated by the intersection of chance and the divine. His own oracle of choice was the *I Ching,* a Chinese fortune-telling ritual, which to him was "a method of exploring the unconscious." By counting forty-nine yarrow sticks, the player receives a pattern of short and long lines that spells out one of sixty-four ideograms, each with a different significance.

To explain how this chance system could be anything other than nonsensical, Jung came up in the 1950s, in his introduction to an English translation of the *I Ching*, with the term "synchronicity": "Synchronicity takes the coincidence of events in space and time as meaning something more than mere chance."

Using the simpler method of *I Ching* consultation—tossing three pennies, with heads as yin and tails as yang—I again asked of the cosmic lottery, this time oriental rather than occidental, about the progress of this book. I wound up with a six-line hexagram, *kuai*, for "Breakthrough," which is always a plus for a writer. So I wasn't doing badly delving into the unconscious that day; I felt I was holding my own against the house. This kind of subjective interpretation reminded me of a Rorschach test: the smudges of black inkblot designs used for personality evaluation, in which one participant might see a swan in flight and someone else a rain cloud.

The contemporary author Deepak Chopra has taken up the theory of synchronicity where Jung left off. He repackaged the psychologist's term as "SynchroDestiny" and made the notion more proactive and practical. I attended Chopra's seminar "SynchroDestiny—Enlightened Leadership for Personal and Professional Success" a few years ago at the Chopra Center in La Jolla, California. He told the group of his feeling that coincidences were actually complex signals from the universe rather than random accidents. He gave as examples two strangers meeting on a train and discovering they have the same name or phone number, or being seated at a dinner next to someone who leads to your next business opportunity, or any sequence of events that takes place and is exactly what is needed to reach an outcome.

The hunch here is that there are no accidents—that everyone you meet, every phone call you receive, every random act of kindness that comes your way is a significant clue or plot point in your life. Of course, looking obsessively for signs can become its own madness. I knew a young woman who went around the bend into a kind of late-night-television lunacy, always looking for omens and signs, not to mention UFOs and ghosts. But taken as an "as if" game to be played with the people and events in our daily life, this activity can lead to lucky results, or to what Chopra called "success." If nothing else, we begin to pay attention.

One evening I was shopping at my usual market when I ran into a prominent playwright I hadn't seen in several years. He asked what I was up to, so I told him that I was actually flying to Iowa the next day to visit a cloister of contemplative nuns. Rather than giving me the blank look I expected, he correctly guessed the name of the obscure, isolated convent of two dozen sisters on the banks of the Mississippi River that was my destination. "My cousin is the mother superior of that community," he informed me. I was visiting as a journalist, and as the nuns led a basically silent life, they had been a bit resistant to the planned interview. By the next afternoon when I arrived, the playwright had called his cousin the abbess, and the doors of communication were opened wide. Because of the unlikely coincidence of the chance encounter, we all seemed convinced that the universe must have had some design in our meeting together.

In the ancient Greek system, no one god is overplayed. Nevertheless, looking for evidence of the stirring of the hand (or angelic wings) of Hermes in daily events can become quite absorbing. Shifting our antennae to expect meaning in random events is a distillation of much of the wisdom of the East. Oriental thought has taught us much about the impinging of mind and perception on so-called objective reality. Even if not finally scientifically true—and who knows?—the approach to people and events as full of significance is at once calming and invigorating, and may very well lead to epiphanies of the Luck-Bringing Messenger.

HERMENEUTIC EXERCISE #3

During a twenty-four-hour period, assume that everything that happens to you is meant to be and that everyone you meet is a messenger from the cosmic scheme of things. You may need to put a few Post-it notes on the telephone and the computer, or carry a note in your pocket, reminding you that your phone calls or meetings that day are especially significant.

During my twenty-four-hour period of keeping my antennae up, I followed through on a few e-mails or phone calls I might have let slide. One that caused me to make a right turn artistically was an e-mail with an attachment from an ex-student. I'd been vacillating recently between two different short story ideas. Just as I was lost in this thought balloon, my "You've Got Mail" announcement went off. A student I hadn't heard from in several years had sent me an indiscreet confessional tale involving an irresistible mix of bodybuilding, motel rooms, frat houses, and bisexuality. I decided to take the e-mail as a sign, and within a few hours had written my story with him as a central character. Writers and artists have made many stories and paintings by treating such random events as clues rather than accidents. (In Greek mythology, Hermes is pointedly the half brother of Hephaestus, the god of creativity. More on him in the next chapter.)

Walking down the street a few hours later, I ran into Constantine. (Yes, he is Greek, with long, wavy brown hair.) I had not seen him in about fifteen years. "Are you married?" I asked after some minutes of conversation, perplexedly noticing the gold wedding band on his finger. "No," he said. "It was my grandmother's. But it was a bone of contention with my ex. And it sure does confuse people. I'm just willful and stubborn and haven't taken it off." A few flirtatious minutes later, he took off the ring and slipped it in his pocket. "Thanks for giving me the inspiration to finally take it off," he said boldly. Just call me Hermes, I thought, not feeling I'd really said anything to inspire the gesture. (We are just as often unaware messengers as we are the recipients of messages.) We then went our separate ways in the bright August sunlight, though not before exchanging numbers, with a plan to reconnect.

A DATE WITH HERMES

A date with Hermes should always have a good-omen feeling. Rather than imposing some activity on yourself, wait and see what comes your way. By giving up control, you may find you have an even more solid footing in a world in constant motion.

As I was doing my Hermeneutic exercises, Pastor Bob, my minister friend who had weighed in earlier on the affinity of dating and brushes with divinity, e-mailed me to ask if I'd like to visit his family's place on Cape Cod for a couple of days. The coincidence of an invitation to go on a journey—the provenance of Hermes—as well as the obvious association of Pastor Bob with God (the target suggested by my recent session with runes), only strengthened my impulse to type back a quick yes.

Our trip paid homage to Hermes by utilizing an entire catalogue of forms of transportation. (I was reminded of the catalogue in the *Iliad* of the Achaean ships lined up like a cavalcade of every make of car.) Pastor Bob borrowed a friend's generic beat-up Mazda for the ride up. We used his parents' Saab for a day trip to Provincetown, on the north tip of the Cape. I took a bus for six hours to get back to Manhattan. The sweetest transport of all was the family sailboat, in which we scudded across Nantucket Sound on a golden late afternoon when the water was wine dark. I learned the two-handed skill of pulling in and letting out sails. Bob looked every bit a New England WASP, with sandy hair, blue eyes, and freckled skin, his adolescent summers living on the sea obvious in the casual, familiar way he handled rope, rudder, and sails.

Our afternoon Provincetown expedition turned out, unexpectedly, to be the occasion of the town's annual parade. "This doesn't look like anybody's hometown," I said, gazing down Commercial Street into an oncoming series of floats, mainly a pageant of gay bar advertisements, while white confetti fluttered down, as well as colored metal necklaces flung from wooden balconies. Even though there was a small-town post office, several ornate Victorian homes, and a flock of seagulls flying out to sea, the ambience didn't seem at all New England: lots of middle-aged, bald, frat-type guys were roaring, offset by RuPaul-style drag queens. I felt I was at a pledge weekend at Penn State or a Mardi Gras festival in New Orleans. One entire posse from a bed-and-breakfast had chosen to go Greek, in either white togas and laurel wreaths or animal-skin skirts and horns.

Hermes was at work in an almost comic pileup of chance meetings. I'd mentioned before arriving that a friend I hadn't seen in ten years had opened a restaurant in Provincetown, and another writer friend was now living there as well. When we randomly pulled into an Italian sandwich shop, I didn't even recognize at first the handsome gray-haired guy walking down the aisle, who turned out to be just that first friend. A few hours later, the writer came sauntering toward me on Commercial Street. Eventually I had conversations with two other authors I knew, as well as with a participant from my seminar in Big Sur. My own necklace of colored metal beads now wrapped around my wrist, I eventually spoke with at least three other surprise visitors. "What a coincidence" was the mantra of the day.

"You saw everybody you knew in the world, it seemed today," said Bob, pretending annoyance, as we drove home in a drizzle, the windshield wiper on slow speed and the radio tuned into a sixties rock station. "I come up here every summer, and I didn't see anybody I knew. It must be partly intention . . . the Hermes thing."

"Possible," I allowed.

That night a wind kept blowing my creaking wooden door open. Bob and I were in adjoining bedrooms on the second floor of the pre–Civil War section of the main gray-shingled house. Each time the door interrupted my sleep, I heard a "Hello" whispered by the wind-and-door combination and I would yell out as if I'd seen a ghost.

The third time, Bob appeared in his white boxers in silhouette in the doorway, his face lit by the full moon. "What's wrong? You afraid? Want me to sleep with you?"

I did. After I heard his childhood stories about the possible haunting of the house, he was asleep. Even I was too tired, finally, for mystic musings on invisible presences or communications from the beyond. All I had left was a residue of what the poet Wallace Stevens, in a fortunate phrase that could well belong in a (modernized) Homeric hymn to Hermes, called "the pleasures of merely circulating."

HERMENEUTIC EXERCISES

1. Create new workouts for yourself, including physical, personal, and social challenges.

2. Identify your own posse by making a list or drawing a map. See how many different kinds of close relationships you have, and how—or if—they overlap and intersect.

3. During a twenty-four-hour period, assume that everything that happens to you is meant to be and that everyone you meet is a messenger from the cosmic scheme of things.

Four

HEPHAESTUS
THE GOD OF CREATIVITY

Hephaestus is the suffering artist. Physically, he's a wreck. He's crippled in both legs, so he has to hobble on a pair of gold crutches. Since his feet are screwed on backward, he can propel himself forward only through a rolling motion of his entire body like a Catherine wheel. With its ugliness, his face is a stop sign that brings everyone to a sudden halt. From limping in such a disfiguring fashion for so long, he's hunchbacked, with his shoulders drawn up around his ears like an ape's. His lack of symmetry is made all the more striking by contrast with the perfection of his fellow Olympian gods and goddesses, supermodels all.

Emotionally, Hephaestus has good reason to be disturbed. He was the original abused child. Though widely considered the son of Zeus and Hera, he was much more of a mama's boy.

In some stories, Hera cloned him from her own thigh, as Zeus did Dionysus. But this time, the result was less pleasing. Faced with the ugly mug of her creation, Hera cast the baby down into the deepest seas, where he was saved only through the kindness of sea goddesses, who helped raise him—much like his brother Dionysus, who spent his childhood in a nymph's grotto, disguised in Barbie doll clothes, hiding out from Hera.

Zeus behaved worse than Hera. When the orphaned Hephaestus made his way back up to Olympus, he sided with his mother in one of those brawls that characterized his parents' relationship. As Homer tells the story in Book 1 of the *Iliad*, Hephaestus—fearing that his parents were going to fight in choosing sides in the battle over Troy—fetched Hera a cup of nectar, trying to get her to calm down. He reminded her how his father, Zeus, in a fit of domestic violence, had once smacked him down, hurling him onto a Greek island far below, causing the crash responsible for his two cracked legs:

> *There was a time once before now I was minded to help you,*
> *And he caught me by the foot and threw me from the magic*
>   *threshold,*
> *And all day long I dropped helpless, and about sunset*
> *I landed in Lemnos, and there was not much life left in me.*
>
> (LATTIMORE TRANSLATION)

Hephaestus's crippled legs are the only imperfection in the otherwise flawless virtual body of the Greek pantheon. If Hermes has fine shins, his legs matched only by his enviable penis, replicated over and over in bronze Oscar statues of herms, Hephaestus was a cuckold and often impotent. He was the only one of the Greek gods who wasn't cock of his walk. His greatest love was the source of his greatest torture. He was married to Aphrodite, the stunningly beautiful and desirable goddess of love. But she was forever cheating on him with his brother Ares, the macho god of war.

Yet Hephaestus got even: he became a great artist. As his skills grew, this god of craftsmanship, blacksmithing, and metalworking couldn't resist punishing the women who most emasculated him, his mother and his wife. For his mother, he designed a magnificent gold throne that sadistically trapped her by automatically snapping manacles on her wrists and ankles when she sat down. (Dionysus had to get him drunk to release her.) Hephaestus designed a similar S&M bondage device to catch Ares and Aphrodite in the act. He crafted a bed that entangled them overnight in a bronze net. Yet the next day when Aphrodite slapped her husband with divorce papers, he slunk away with his ego between his legs.

Hephaestus got his revenge by living well. He became fabulous. His studio was a cross between Andy Warhol's Factory and Hugh Hefner's Playboy Mansion. His name in ancient Greek meaning "fire" (its Latin translation was Vulcan), Hephaestus set up shop in the volcanoes of Mt. Aetna and Mt. Vesuvius. Among his first creations were lovely female interns made of gold who assisted him with his work. Besides these talking Barbarella robots, he built tripods (chairs and tables) on wheels that navigated the premises by means of artificial intelligence. To his design credit were the brass palaces of the gods. His most famous work was Achilles' shield, in which all of earthly life, framed by heavenly stars, was simulated. After working overtime at his bellows and anvil, black with soot and covered with sweat, according to the modern poet W. H. Auden in "The Shield of Achilles," "The thin-lipped armourer, Hephaestos hobbled away . . ."

Unlike some of his more schizoid relatives, Hephaestus is simple to understand. He was the outcast, the alien, and the nerd. Instead of showing up at school armed to the teeth (as his brother Ares might have done), he transformed his curse into a blessing, pain into pleasure, and suffering into triumph. Though never a gay teenager, he resembled one in having to learn early on to plug in to his own independent power source. Working with a crippling, alienating reality, Hephaestus eventually found himself—to the cumulative amazement of himself, his parents, and the rest of the gods—the center of all beauty.

MEDITATIONS AND EXERCISES

PAIN AND CREATIVITY

Over a stormy Labor Day weekend, fraught with an ominous overload of police sirens and fire engines revving in the station house across the street, I found myself identifying with Hephaestus, regressing into feeling sorry for myself over a brief dating experience from which I'd emerged burned and moping. At the nub of all Hephaestus's created beauty, after all, is pain. But pain is not a wormhole down which many of us voluntarily descend.

Growing in any kind of wisdom or self-reliance is a two-steps-forward, one-step-back process. As a steady reader of self-help books, I'd often had the experience of being encouraged by a book, putting its advice into practice for days or weeks, and then slipping back into forgetfulness. I would need to recharge my batteries by reading a similar message in a similar book. I was startled, humbled, and a bit amused to find the same slippage can occur even for a writer. I sometimes forgot that I had all the insight and technique that I acquired from having written *Finding the Boyfriend Within*. Yet occasionally, I've found myself needing to reread my own book.

A few weeks earlier, one of those skids had begun for me when I'd met Renaldo at the Big Cup, a coffee shop on Eighth Avenue in Chelsea. Or rather, when Renaldo met me. There I was, sipping my café latte, and he drinking his tall raspberry iced tea, when he strode over boldly with a phone number scribbled on a yellow piece of tablet paper in his outstretched palm.

"If you want to go to *Hairspray* on Friday night, let me know," he said in his—as I was to discover—Venezuelan accent. "My friend is having a theater party."

I took him in, stunned. I'd definitely seen Renaldo around: tall, black hair cut short, olive-skinned, usually dressed in boots and gray painter's pants. He was a bit hard to place. As I was later to discover, he worked as a makeup artist in the fashion industry.

I couldn't make the musical . . . though he hadn't really given me a chance that afternoon to tell him so. I did call him on the rainy Saturday afternoon after the play. "Where have you been? Come over now," he said with unusual authority. I did, and we had a romantic afternoon intercut with watching Julia Roberts in *Sleeping with the Enemy,* which was fast fare on a cable channel. I was taking in his compact studio apartment, with bike hung on wall, more pots and pans and kitchenware than books, lots of glossy magazines, when he revealed to me, slipped under the glass cover of a coffee table, my own publicity shot for a book promotion, clipped from a magazine a few years back.

"I told my friend, 'See this guy, I'm gonna sleep with him,'" Renaldo bragged to me. I have to admit to taking a brief, knowing, psychic half step backward at that moment, but decided to pretend all was well.

I thrived for a couple of weeks in the hothouse of attention that was Renaldo's apartment. His cell phone number seemed always available for my calls. He would pick up instantly. He invited me to dinner almost every night and cooked serious food: skirt steak, steamed lobster, chicken paella. My only choice in the matter was to say no as much as yes, to keep the window

cracked a comfortable bit. I still, for instance, was never convinced his English was all there, or that he understood, or was
listening, to a word I said. Whenever I did say no, though, his
temper showed. Latin passion, I thought to myself. Also, if I
was telling him of any plan or obligation, his answer, with a big,
sexy smile, would be, "Did I tell you that you could?"

Then came the reversal, in the form of his blond Icelandic
friend, a male model, who was arriving to stay for a few weeks.
An old boyfriend, down on his luck, was the story. Where will he
sleep? I wondered. In the single couch-bed with Renaldo?
Along with the appearance of Sven came a sharp change in the
emotional climate. Renaldo's cell phone, obviously equipped
with caller ID, never picked up again when I dialed. Renaldo
visited my apartment, instead of the other way around, and had
always eaten when we met. After his final, truncated visit, he
was on his way to a very important work appointment, planning
a shoot, though the time was Saturday night at ten o'clock.

The crunch in this dynamic—a commonplace in neurotic, as
opposed to authentic, entanglement—was that I was *just* finally
beginning to enjoy our TV-lit dinners. I was *just* beginning to
imagine a South American vacation. Sensing that something
was off, I left a message of the "Anything wrong?" variety. I received one back, a growl that went something like, "I love hanging out with you, but you're never around, and I had to go see
friends for work . . . I'm too old to play games."

This (still, to me) inexplicable halt in the straight-to-cable
movie of our romance registered as an emotional "Ouch!" Its
dark tone, real or imaginary, and my own certainty that I didn't
have all the information to explain these goings-on bothered me
for nearly twenty-four hours. I wallowed in my funk. Sometime

during the next afternoon, though, I finally stopped envisioning a caricature of Renaldo's disapproving face. I stopped hearing our phone messages—or my own melodramatic version of them—replayed in the microcassette recorder in my head. Instead, I visualized a black paint smudge smeared across a white page, then another, then a nimbus of orange around the black hole. I could almost smell the waxy scent of finger paints, which I had not smelled in decades.

So I took a walk to Pearl Paint on Canal Street, luckily open on a holiday weekend, where I bought a Sargent's washable finger paints kit of eight nontoxic colors and a few extra sheets of glossy paper. The instructions recommended standing up, which I did, spreading the sheets over the kitchen table, while listening to Moby's melodic-techno CD *Play.* After a few swipes, astonished at the tang of the colors they were offering— pomegranate red, chocolate pudding brown, tapioca yellow—I began to funnel feeling through my fingers. Most thankful for the jet black, I expressed my adult emotions through juvenile materials. After about thirty minutes, I'd pretty much, in the words of the very un-Mobylike song from *South Pacific,* "washed that man right out of my hair."

The man, in this case, was Renaldo. Or my imaginary Renaldo, since the more I thought about our truncated romance, which grew fainter with every swathe of sun yellow or sky blue, the fainter the drama grew. The truth was that I had never felt we were on the same page. I bore much responsibility for never voicing my committed attraction. And I was not a judge who was ever going to get him to turn over the evidence, if there was any—which he never did. Even if he and Sven were this month's fashion photographer's ideal pairing of brunette and blond, Latino and Nordic—who cares? I was back: a dynamo of mixed feelings, including confidence, the confidence of someone who could simply smear kindergarten orange over black without even needing the excuse of Halloween.

In this reversal, I felt the deft hand of Hephaestus at work. He's the god who operates by reversals, after all, turning pain into beauty or even comedy. The therapy of creativity often involves taking a dark, primal situation—including, for Hephaestus, parental abuse and emotional and sexual abandonment by a lover, not to mention physical malady—and turning the feeling around. In the first book of the *Iliad*, Homer tellingly presents the slapstick scene of a deadly serious conference of gods on Mount Olympus—a sort of meeting of the security council—which Hephaestus characteristically, and for the good of everyone involved, breaks up into hiccups of giggles by limping around, pouring wine, mimicking the flaunting of pectorals by the original trophy boy, Ganymede, beloved of Zeus:

> *But among the blessed immortals uncontrollable laughter*
> *Went up as they saw Hephaistos bustling about the palace.*
> (LATTIMORE TRANSLATION)

HEPHAESTIAN EXERCISE #1

Find a creative activity that seems spontaneous, childish, or out of character. Try this activity when you're feeling frustrated, angry, or depressed. Stick with activities that prove reliable at turning pain into pleasure.

Among the amateur creative activities taken up by some of my friends, or friends of friends:

- Knitting
- Underwater photography
- Argentine tango
- Mexican cooking
- Country-Western singing
- Life drawing

CREATIVE DATING

Creativity these days, of course, is for everyone, not just gods or royals. Instinctively, we all know it's crucial for our well-being. I was standing idly at a benefit cocktail party one evening when the managing editor of a prominent magazine walked up to me. We each asked politely, what the other was doing. "I'm still working away at the magazine," he replied. "The last time we talked, about a year ago, I told you how I was going to try to open up a wedge of creativity in my life. But seeing you here is a reminder that I still haven't done so."

We express this nearly universal sense of the importance of creativity in our choice of heroes. Back in Homer's day, the hero of heroes was the warrior or king, or best of all, the warrior-king. No one beat Achilles for popularity. In our own time, we rarely turn to generals for our heroes. A lot of recent biopics are about artists, instead: Picasso, Pollock, Basquiat, and Frida Kahlo. Hephaestus as the tortured artist has a particularly modern feeling tone. He's the antigod; his vulnerability is his greatest power. In his model of overcoming adversity through beauty rather than strength, he probably can grant us the most immediate, in-the-moment gratification as well.

Not only is creativity now popular—a shift hinted at wittily in the phrase "Pop Art," associated with Andy Warhol—but "Be creative!" has become an injunction not just in the arts but in business, sports, and social life as well. Hiding in plain sight on the cusp of social life and our most intimate, personal life lies dating, an everyday (or night) pastime that might well be the most creative of human encounters, a veritable mystery cult of love and intellectual stimulation. Yet dating too often seems stuck, instead, in a model of old business: two people interviewing each other across a desk of a café table. (Or in the case of me and Renaldo, dispensing with the interview altogether.) Dating is a prime example of a popular activity that could well be reinvented by an infusion of the table-turning, creative energy of Hephaestus.

"Isn't dating passé?" my barber asked recently, while cutting my hair cowboy-style, leaving on the sideburns. "I stopped dating a long time ago. It's like a cliché. Anybody who sits in this chair and starts telling me about their dating experiences tells me a horror story. What's the point? Dating is for teenagers. The idea of two grown men all anxious and nervous about whether they're gonna like or be liked seems ludicrous. I have more important things to do." For my barber, what began as a pleasure had become a pain.

Dating as an extreme—or not extreme enough—sport is not confined to gays, of course. Another friend told me recently of attending an evening at a gay bar in the East Village set up for power dating, a phenomenon widely popular in the straight clubs that was being launched as an experiment in this venue. He described a long counter with men on both sides, and a metallic-sounding buzzer timed to sound every few minutes. During these truncated segments, partners would ask each other a list of basic questions that were important to them in choosing a mate: "What do you do?" "Where do you live?" "Do you own, or rent?" "What are you into?" Having checked off the appropriate squares on their own tip sheet, they would move to their next partner. By the end of one session, the power daters would have a list of candidates to consider for round two—a personal get-together.

The advanced dating game my friend described at least had the advantage of being creative, of trying to do *something* to refresh the convention. Yet superpracticality can also induce superanxiety. In trying to think outside the box, the power-dating inventors might well have wound up designing a stark cage. Even in the more standard version of a date as an information-gathering mission, the endgame is often construed as trying to match up with someone who fits our preexisting job description for them. No one wastes time with those whose numbers are off the chart. But this way of being together unfortunately leaves out all the surprises that lie on either side of the application form.

The poet Emily Dickinson wrote, "Truth in circuit lies." Well, intimacy may in circuit lie as well. And this circling is just how creativity works—whether in writing a poem or story, or in doing business, or in going on a date. If I'm experiencing writer's block, I often just scribble down random words and thoughts that pop into my head for a few pages without censoring. By looking away, I tend to find an opening more surely than by marching ahead. Nearly everyone has had the experience of trying to remember a name, and after giving up, while doing something unrelated, having the name pop into his head. Likewise in dating, the best way to get to the heart of the matter is often to proceed sideways.

The obvious way to have a creative date is to pair up for a creative activity. I had just such a date with Constantine, whom I had run into at the sunny intersection—of the street and in his life—a few weeks earlier. "It's me, Constantine . . . the Greek," he'd left as his teasing phone message, knowing my involvement with ancient Greece, leaving off the word "god" apparently out of (false?) humility. Then he added, surprisingly: "Want to get together and lay down some dance tracks? I have all the equipment, and programs." By laying down dance tracks he meant composing music with a computer rather than a traditional guitar, keyboard, or set of drums.

A few nights later, full of question marks, I showed up at his apartment in the Colonnades building, opposite the Public Theater—a fitting location, as he's an actor. Dressed down in green cargo shorts, khaki T-shirt, and Teva sandals, his rocky nose inspiring me with archaic fantasies, Constantine proceeded to a counter that was set with a daunting array of instruments: keyboard, computer screen, recording device, and a pile of colored floppies, each containing drumrolls, sound effects, or musical scales in different keys.

"This is the humblest hardware you can possibly have, believe me," he explained, reacting to my startled look as he swiveled into place on a gray conductor's chair.

"It looks like the control panel of a commercial jet," I shot back. "What's creative about that?"

The act of composing electronically consisted mostly of picking and choosing. Constantine would play two different rhythm tracks and say, "Which one do you like? Pick one." I would, and my choice, entered by code, would appear on the flat screen, transposed into a square of red or green on a gray grid. Constantine taped the sound, which was then transposed into a pattern replayed on a black key of the keyboard, and soon my claps were a deep beat worthy of heavy house music.

"What I'm doing with you is simpler than I'd do on my own, less like coming up with a genius commercial dance track," he said in his gravelly voice, inflected by Long Island, where he'd grown up with his first-generation immigrant parents from Sparta. "But it's better. Usually I get stuck because it's not perfect. Then I go out and have sex or something. But with you hanging out here, I'm less a perfectionist. I'm just putting stuff down . . . Maybe you should always sit here when I make music."

Soon after 1 A.M., we parted with a hug. I wished Constantine good luck in L.A., where he was flying in two days to try out for TV pilots and to meet a new manager. As I walked down a few floors of stairs, holding the disk imprinted with our creation, I thought how we'd done more than lay down dance tracks. I'd gotten to know Constantine in a way I never would have if our reacquainting date had been set at a table at a coffee shop—with me tabulating in my head our age differential, or specific sexual predilections, or relationship histories. Music had distracted me from my own cliché of dating. And Hephaestus had been paid his due because, as Constantine pointed out, collaboration can often be one of the best triggers for creativity. It's certainly an inspiring pretext for a date.

HEPHAESTIAN EXERCISE #2

Invite a friend or partner on a creative date. If you know someone who practices an art or craft, ask if he'd give you a beginner's lesson. If not, go for an activity at which both of you are beginners.

Some creative activities that can be done together:

- Acting class
- Practicing the art of massage
- Team cooking
- Trapeze class

Dating is not simply for the young or the infatuated (though they might be the most likely to overlook its downside and come away feeling the rush of beginner's luck). The secret to jump-starting friendships and long-term relationships, as well, is creative dating. You don't need to limit this notion of being creative—as European aristocrats did in the eighteenth century—to going out to look at natural vistas through golden frames, making your own pictures, as it were. That is, you don't *have* to be arty.

When I was talking with a friend about the possibility of creative dating, she said, "I haven't been on a date in so long."

"Well, maybe you should start," I said.

"Errgh," she replied.

"The thing about a creative date," I went on, "is that even if it doesn't work out, you still have fun."

"That's a good way of looking at it," she allowed.

Online dating has the advantage of at least updating the format. Potential partners can interview each other across cyberspace rather than across a table. Matchmaking can be plugged-in rather than unplugged. By using instant messages, e-mails, or websites designed for arranging blind dates, helped along by graphic images or electronic self-portraits done with digital cameras, players have the titillation of turning what was painful into more of a game. And gone is the secondhand smoke of bars. But once you're face-to-face with your mysterious screen name of a stranger, you still have the choice of where to go, what to do. A Starbucks coffee date is not the solution to every romantic mystery.

If you feel stuck about how to best enliven a scheduled date, the gods can help. All of the gods introduced so far embody qualities that not only enhance our interior life but can do the same for our social life. When next wondering how to plan an evening with someone, do your own postmodern version of invoking the gods by scrolling down the list of deities until you're inspired with an activity. You've done solo dates with Greek gods. Now do three-ways. Leaving aside for the moment the unique pleasure of selfless accession to the needs of a loved one, the test of a good date is: you'd be glad to have ridden that bike or hiked that trail anyway. Dates often work best when thought of as ends in themselves, rather than means to an end.

Among possible dates inspired by the qualities of the Greek gods:

An Apollonian-style date
  Going to a play
  Reading aloud to each other

A Dionysian-style date
Going to a rock concert
Dressing up together for a Halloween parade or party

A Hermeneutic-style date
Spending a week on a Caribbean cruise
Skiing for a weekend in Vermont

A DATE WITH HEPHAESTUS

For a solo date with Hephaestus, be creative—not just in the doing but in the selecting. Choose activities that are unfamiliar to you. If you're already a master at one art, try another. Notice any reverb effect: an evening of choral singing might open a new avenue in a movie script or play you've been writing.

The gods often hide in plain sight. For my date with Hephaestus—a solo creative date—I stepped into the Koho School of Sumi-E, offering japanese brush painting classes. I'd walked by this quiet, unprepossessing shop at the corner of my street every day for four years, occasionally noting the calm Buddha statue in its window. Yet the school remained for me a sidebar in the neighborhood.

On the evening of September 11, 2002, the first anniversary of the destruction of the World Trade Center, I finally stopped by for a group class with the teacher, a Japanese woman, Koho Yamamoto, apparently in her sixties. "You are my neighbor," she said with a lilting accent, charging me a few dollars less. "I have been here in this location thirty years." At this introductory two-hour class, from six-thirty until eight-thirty, with three other students—two men in suits and a female publicist, obviously all just off work—I discovered that we were to address Ms. Yamamoto as "Sensei," or Master.

That evening, at least, her face was as pale as the white paper drawn on by the more advanced students, her eyes made up with black ink as dark and expressionist as the strokes of their brushes. She wore a black skirt and a green blouse seemingly made from parchment, or tissue. In a casual but evidently standard ritual, she pushed the button on a boom box from which issued bamboo flute music. Having prepared green tea, she passed the cups around politely.

"As soon as you begin to prepare the *sumi-e,* you are already painting," she first told me, while pouring water in a black box and scraping it with a wooden block covered in gold calligraphic lettering. By pressing and pressing, the mixture of ink and water grew blacker. "I do about twenty times, either circles, or straight," she said, pushing into the motion like someone laundering a difficult garment.

"Then you hold your brush like chopsticks," she said, as she guided my hand for the first few strokes. "You hold your breath for all three strokes. Stop, go. Stop, go. Stop, go." A stack of half sheets of the *New York Times* was piled next to me as worksheets. On a stand in front, my model: a rendition of a black bamboo stick with branches and leaves.

Ms. Yamamoto went around with a light touch, most of her sentences inflected with humor, and dealt with everyone's issues. The more advanced the student, the tougher the advice.

"Oh, you paint too much with your arm. You will feel pain. Just paint lightly, with the tip of your hand," she said to the gentleman next to me, who had brought a gift for all of us of a pistachio green Japanese sponge cake with beige icing from his wife's tea shop on Fifth Avenue.

"Too free, too free, too crazy," was her opinion of my own jazzy bamboo shoot with its branches, which were disconnected cross-hatching, like antennae on the roofs of houses. "If you make the node too thick, looks like telephone pole."

Clarity, release, and a tickled sense of having done something special did finally kick in. The magic of this technique, relying (according to her advertising pamphlet) on "the finest traditions of Far Eastern Art and Zen philosophy," was to feel that we were not just learning to make exotic shapes, the visual equivalent of haiku, but learning something valuable and rare about our own heaviness or lightness, our pride or distraction. We were transformed by the self-knowledge generated through making these tiny lines and swatches.

Hephaestus is a divinity of the pantheon, and so a successful date with him might yield spiritual benefits as well as simple pleasures. I realized along the way that our sensei was delivering insights steadily, one after another, in the form of her aesthetic judgments. She was reading us. For instance, after guiding someone's hand through a leaf brush stroke: "I can't hold your hand all through life." Certainly in this discipline, and with this incisive teacher, the spirituality, as well as the therapy, in creativity was stressed perhaps more than in some other activities.

"You want to go to candlelight service?" Ms. Yamamoto asked the publicist as the session was being brought delicately to its close and we lined up to wash our brushes in a deep porcelain sink stained with decades of paint.

"You may come back whenever you feel ready," she said as a good-bye to me, with a dignified nod.

As we stepped out into the street, crowds of people were holding unlit candles on their way to a vigil at the nearby firehouse. The occasion was a commemoration of firefighters who had lost their lives at the towers, which used to loom visibly at the end of our street like a vertical high-rise of trillions of such candles.

I felt the difference in that single step between Ares, the god of war, presented by the ancient Greeks as such a cowardly thug, the force responsible for political acts of violence, and his much more inspiring brother Hephaestus, who could take the form of a Japanese lady with ivory hands able to make everyone feel transformed, as if they were as light as a tree's branch.

Crossing the street, I ran into my neighbor Annie, an artist. She was returning from her own studio, a few doors down, where she'd just finished a silk screen. I was holding my pile of worksheets, the newsprint now covered with broad black strokes and fine black dashes.

"Oh, these are nice, I think you have a talent for this," Annie said, squinting at the sheets, curbside, beneath the lit moon of a streetlamp. (Everything had gone oriental in my perception by then.) "I feel this will lead you somewhere. Not to calligraphy, maybe, but to a story about a crazy calligrapher or something."

Then she added, with a prescience that made me wonder, in my altered state, if she *knew* I was on a date with Hephaestus: "I'm glad to have run into you tonight, at such a creative moment."

HEPHAESTIAN EXERCISES

1. Find a creative activity that seems spontaneous, childish, or out of character. Try this activity when you're feeling frustrated, angry, or depressed.

2. Invite a friend or partner on a creative date.

Five

EROS
THE GOD OF LOVE

As a contemporary devotee of Eros, the male god of love and desire, Madonna has reinvented her look, sound, and message more often than any other popular performer. An exuberant lover of the material world in all its manifestations, she dripped diamonds as a "material girl." In her *Sex* book, partially photographed at the sleazy male burlesque the Gaiety Theatre in midtown Manhattan, she was all whips and chains and black rubber cat suits. On the *Ray of Light* CD, she assumed the lotus position to sing of the spiritual light of love, evolving into a translucent philosopher of the bedroom.

Like the remix diva of *Erotica,* the original god Eros evolved radically in look and character, too, his own reinventions paralleling the three main eras of ancient Greek history—the archaic, the classical, and the Hellenistic. Always an exception in the standard lineup of gods, Eros was considered (1) too deep and powerful to be whittled down even to the size of a super-hero of a god; *or* (2) too mischievous to be treated as more than an unruly offspring of Aphrodite, the goddess of love, and of any of an entire paternity suit of gods; *or* (3) subtle and complex enough to be understood only by the leading philosophical minds. Adding the all-important element of heart to the mix, though, he always lit up the life of the Greek pantheon.

The first and most ancient of his appearances was that of the archaic Eros, the god of primal love worshiped by Orphic cults, who was as extravagant as a drag queen at the Love Ball. This Eros was a fantastic mythological creature, a double-sexed be-ing, woman on the front, man on the back, who emerged from the silver egg of Night with four eyes, four horns, and golden wings, roaring like a bull and bellowing like a lion. His/her first impulse was to reach back into the bottomless egg as if it were a handbag and draw forth from its black, velvety depths the en-tire world, beginning with Oceanus (the male principle of the ocean) and Tethys (the female principle of the sea)—the first couple to marry, as their chemistry was so good. From their union, the human race was eventually created. During this ini-tial phase of Eros's development, to quote the Beatles, as cov-ered in *Moulin Rouge:* "All you need is love." Love was cosmic and metaphysical. Love made the world go round. Everything in the world was created from love.

The second appearance of Eros, among the classical Greeks, came closest to the greeting-card Cupid of the later Romans—the pink, dimpled, pudgy little boy with a sheath full of arrows. But this classical Eros, the irrationally exuberant god of roman-tic love, was more of a troubled (and troubling) adolescent in skintight jeans, with a pocketknife, a cigarette lighter, a blind-fold, and miles of attitude. He could pierce and he could burn. A delinquent teenager, his paternity is in dispute. Eros comes from a broken home. But generally Aphrodite, the goddess of love, is accepted as his mom. His absentee dad was most likely Ares, the god of war. This coupling makes sense as Eros's sym-bols, his arrows and torch, are weapons, like those used by Ares, only in his case for love, not war. He shoots his arrows through the eyes, signifying that romantic love often begins at first sight.

The classical Eros became a stand-in, or proxy, as the male god of love as well. In ancient Greek, the word *aphrodisia* meant "things of Aphrodite" and the verb for getting laid was *aphrodisiazein*. The original plan for the family corporation of Love stipulated that Aphrodite would manage the erogenous zone, or G-spot, while Eros would concentrate on the obses-sive focusing of desire on one person, or falling in love. As time went on, according to some scholars, love was restructured: Aphrodite oversaw all heterosexual passion, Eros all homosex-ual passion. As the first century B.C. poet Meleager wrote in a giggle of a paragraph:

> Aphrodite, female . . . , ignites the fire that makes one mad for a woman, but Eros himself holds the reins of male desire. Which way am I to incline? To the boy or to his mother? I declare that even Aphrodite herself will say: "The bold lad is the winner!"
>
> (DOVER TRANSLATION)

His third incarnation, as the Eros of Socrates and Plato and of the later, Hellenistic philosophers, was the most sublime of all. The Hellenistic Eros shows us the spiritual face of love, or what we often call platonic love. The manual for understanding this subtle Eros, broken up as he is in electrons of pure thought, was Plato's *Symposium,* an account of a dinner party that took place in Athens at the home of the avant-garde playwright Agathon in 416 B.C. to celebrate his winning the equivalent of a Tony for his tragedy that season. The guests were all men, re-clining on couches, who decided, after dessert, to offer wine toasts to Eros. Going around in turn, their toasts, or hymns to Eros, grew into a philosophical debate about the nature of erotic love.

Socrates, of course, blew everyone away. He uncovered, in the longing of Eros for beauty, a secret recipe for mature love. He revealed how this Peter Pan might actually grow up. The growth curve, according to Socrates, begins with desiring one boy's body, then another's, then inner beauty in a boy or a man, until finally there unfolds the desire of the soul for beauty itself:

> When someone goes up by these stages, through loving boys in the correct way, and begins to catch sight of that beauty, he has come close to reaching the goal . . . . Like someone using a staircase, he should go from one to two and from two to all beautiful bodies, and from beautiful bodies to beautiful practices, and from practices to beau-tiful forms of learning.
>
> (CHRISTOPHER GILL TRANSLATION)

Over the centuries the ancient Greeks, grappling with the elusive nature of love, created a composite drawing, like a po-lice sketch, of this most wanted of gods. In the layering and complexity of their portrait—which required centuries of touching up—was much truth. Anyone who's had an embodied Eros in his own life knows how changeable and layered a lover can be. Sometimes he's so "other" that you forget his name. Sometimes he's a muscular body wrapped in revealing white sheets. And then there are those memorable, shared moments of looking into each other's eyes and feeling soulful. Eros is the god responsible for this deep commingling of light and dark, love and desire, which takes place in the normal heart.

MEDITATIONS AND EXERCISES

PRIMAL LOVE

We're used to doing endless detective work on the mystery of love. Some instinct or clue tells us that love is crucial to our well-being and happiness. The books written on the topic lined up on self-help shelves reinforce this assumption—Marianne Williamson's title is *A Return to Love;* Byron Katie's, *Loving What Is.* And there are many more. Their sheer number attests to the deep pull of this force. Yet these writers' precursors, the archaic Greeks, were in a way the most profound, for all of the different theories of love can be contained in their original sense of love as the magnetic force of attraction responsible for the creation of everything in the world. As the poet Allen Ginsberg used to say, "First thought, best thought."

Certainly no imperative occurs more often in literature in all languages than some version of "Listen to your heart." As Sir Philip Sidney breaks open his Renaissance sequence of sonnets: "Fool! said my Muse to me, look in thy heart and write." The bottom line of all the exercises in all the self-help books ever written is some version or another of "Look in thy heart." Don Juan, the Yaqui wise man, tells the anthropologist Carlos Castaneda in *Teachings of Don Juan: A Yaqui Way of Knowledge:* "For me there is only the traveling on paths that have heart, on any path that may have heart." Don Juan was simply reaffirming the primacy of Eros.

EROTIC EXERCISE #1

Close your eyes. Take a deep breath. Concentrate on the feeling in your heart, without any thought or words and without following any impulse to act. Stay with the feeling for a few moments.

This basic exercise accomplishes much. When I sit down and tune in to my heart, I'm invariably surprised at how far I've drifted. I may find that I've encircled myself in all sorts of hopeless thinking, which goes nowhere and often leads to feeling bad. Or I discover that stress has created a squeeze box in which the heart rests like a bad science experiment. After a few moments of such sitting, things usually fall into a happier configuration. To put the phenomenon in ancient Greek terms, I've reestablished the priority of Eros, or the heart principle. I'm no longer out of sorts.

A second exercise for bringing home to ourselves the vastness of Eros, its dimensions including everything from the creation of mountains and seas to the simpler pleasures of lovemaking or romantic dinners, is to write a love poem with a capital *L*. Poetry and love have always been related. It's hard to talk about love without bringing in its experts, the poets. In his "Poem Read at Joan Mitchell's," Frank O'Hara wrote of thinking of fellow poet John Ashbery:

> *I think*
> *of John and the nuptial quality*
> *of his verses (he is always marrying the whole world)*

I recently watched a documentary on Joan Mitchell, the New York School painter to whom O'Hara's poem was dedicated. She talked surprisingly of dealing with love in her abstract canvases. She then clarified that the love she was painting was love for "the river" or for "the doggies." This group of poets and artists had obviously experienced Eros in the archaic Greek sense, as the energizer of the big picture. Their take was similar to that of Hesiod, who in his *Theogony,* or *Birth of the Gods,* written in the late eighth or early seventh century B.C., made Eros, "the fairest of the deathless gods," one of the first of four immortal beings and the heart energy responsible for all of creation. Or of Sappho, the seventh century B.C. poet who lived on the island of Lesbos, and wrote in one of her surviving lyric fragments:

> *Eros shook my*
> *mind like a mountain wind falling on oak trees*
> (CARSON TRANSLATION)

EROTIC EXERCISE #2

Write a catalogue poem with "I love . . ." at the top of the page and your list of choices beneath.

In my own catalogue poem, I listed several proper names covering romantic, brotherly, and familial love, as well as some personal, idiosyncratic passions. In my mix, too: natural beauties worthy of the god the Orphic hymns praised as "master of all."

My own love poem included

Coffee
Mom
Going to just about any movie
The sunflowers in the glass pitcher
Larry
Sally
The white noise of traffic
The church bells a block away
Silk boxers
Fall

ROMANTIC LOVE

As patrolled by the punk figure of Eros, romantic turf can be treacherous. People grow touchy here, or insecure, or hot under the collar. I wouldn't want to impose a definition of romance on anyone, including myself. The only constant in exploring romance, though, is that the heart must be active. You can have lots of Dionysian sexual energy aroused by a stranger lurking in the corner, but if the heart doesn't light up, it's not romance. It's lust.

Not everyone is upbeat about romantic love. The French author Stendhal compared love to a virus, which you receive in a virulent dose when young but to which you gradually develop immunity with age. His dismissal of romantic love as a contagion similar to the common cold illustrates the anger or resentment that can be aroused by this controversial feeling. Longing is an important element of romantic love. And with longing inevitably comes frustration. The oscillation between longing and either satisfaction or frustration gives romantic love the quality of a competitive game, the metaphor most used for its description.

But romantic love is a life enhancer, too—especially when experienced with someone else, a brother in love. In one of the telling tales in Greek mythology, Aphrodite complained to the goddess Themis (Law) that her son Eros was stuck in extended adolescence. Themis revealed to her that the cause was his solitude. If he had a brother, her stunted son would begin to grow up. Anterus (Answering Love) was soon born to Ares and Aphrodite, and Eros increased rapidly in size and strength. Eros and Anterus make a nice gay couple. If you have an Anterus in your life, then tapping into erotic love can be done safely as a way to tune up a romantic success story. Anyone who's been in a long-term relationship knows that if there isn't occasional sparking, the wires go dead. Romance with Anterus is more a decision than an obsession. If you're in such a relationship, this myth's for you.

For everyone else, Aphrodite's son is best dealt with as a figure of fun. The best response to his appearance: "Cool!" The general rule: "Use it or lose it." A friend announced that when he reached fifty he stopped going to gay bars: "I retired from the unequal struggle." A woman said to me recently, "As we get older, we get more invisible." The assumption is that the number of hits on our personal website decreases. But the longing remains. Often enough, though, contrary to prejudice, the hits remain, too. A white-haired executive confided to me that he met a young Eastern European Amtrak conductor while on his way home to Long Island. Pretty soon the conductor was sitting next to him with a hand on his thigh.

One of the most erotic novels of the past half century, *The Persian Boy* by Mary Renault, was written surprisingly by a lesbian author imagining the love affair between a Persian eunuch and the conquering Greek king, Alexander the Great. The boy, Bagoas, from whose point of view the historical novel is written, casts himself as a devotee of Eros. He writes, in a mythological steam, when finding his wish fulfilled by being invited for the first time into the bed of Alexander: "Eros had gathered his net in the strong grip of a god, and pulled in his catch, no longer to be defied."

Because of the perennial adolescence of Eros, one sure way to get in touch with erotic longing is through memory. Before September of each high school year, I remember, I'd check my yearbook to figure out which boys I hoped to find in my homeroom that year. Growing up in a preliberation era, I dared not ask my favorite basketball player to the prom. Yet such unrequited longing and pining has made many into true connoisseurs when it comes to the ways of Eros.

EROTIC EXERCISE #3

Titillate yourself by writing down a list of your teenage crushes.

My own list:

- Mark, the basketball player
- Kurt, the hoodlum

- Bobby, my best friend
- Arnie, the paperboy

Two of these figures remain golden blurs in my heart: Mark, the basketball player, and Arnie, the paperboy. My best friend, Bobby, was also, in retrospect, my first boyfriend. We had an erotic relationship for about a year that went on fitfully for a couple of more years, into our middle teens. Kurt I actually met up with again at my tenth high school reunion. By then he'd been divorced and had spent time in the marines. We ended up going home together. Eros was in full flower that evening.

EROTIC EXERCISE #4

List current crushes. If you draw a blank, you can include crushes from movies, sports, or TV.

My crush list:

- Fernando
- Carlos
- CoolSurfer
- Vin Diesel
- The guy downstairs

"Erotic" is often used as an adjective for sex toys: ticklers, vibrators. A popular lube in a tube from Germany is named Eros. So a list of crushes is usually a playful and irresponsible wish list. My own list slants toward Brazilians, one of whom I've never met but is a promised blind date through a friend. The list includes a Yahoo! screen name, an actor in a current movie, and a straight guy. Erotic energy can be its own stimulant, an aphrodisiac for existence itself. But as the myth of Anterus promises us, friendship and love may result from an erotic attraction as well. Surprise, after all, is the M.O. of Eros.

PLATONIC LOVE

Platonic love has developed a bad rep. The image evoked is of guilty virgins lacking in self-knowledge, simple bravery, or curiosity sitting on opposite ends of a couch staring awkwardly at each other. Platonic love is for wimps. In after-school specials, when the girl says she's interested in a platonic relationship, the boy's heart sinks because he knows that means she's not really into him. The only worse insult would be for her to tell him she just wants to be friends.

At his dinner with Agathon, Socrates was hardly giving a handy philosophical excuse for disinterest, a polite exit line from a sticky situation. Nor was he suggesting abstinence, or even the replacement of bed with books. He was using the popular conception of Eros as the god of flirty love to begin to imagine a mature love that would touch what we might call soul. Sure, he was talking about getting beyond bodies, but getting beyond doesn't necessarily mean leaving behind. He was talking of getting beyond personalities, too, in seeing into beauty itself, but insight into what might be called soul isn't necessarily exclusive of people, either.

The meaning of Socrates' speech on love is still debated. His monologue was as much a tenor aria as a logical argument. The Victorian understanding was that he was saying we should abandon romantic love for philosophical study. But many sensitive modern scholars have been arguing instead that this famous disquisition on Eros had *everything* to do with people, rather than being a sermon on just saying no to romantic love. Summing up those moderns on this tetchy issue, Christopher Gill, a translator of *The Symposium,* writes: "In this interpretation, what the passage describes is not the replacement of impersonal love by philosophy, but the deepening of interpersonal love by the lover's growing understanding of the true nature of beauty." Evidence is Socrates' advice that lovers could then share their insights in *logoi,* or discourse, with their boyfriends, indulging in a new kind of philosophical pillow talk.

What Socrates didn't spell out, he acted out. On the night of the *Symposium* dinner, shattering the sublimity of the discourse just spun on the transcendent dimensions of Eros, Alcibiades, according to Plato, showed up at the party drunk, making a surprise entrance like the hustler who appears as the icing on the birthday cake in *The Boys in the Band.* This particular guy-toy, a young Athenian general and politician known for his physical prowess and beauty as well as for some dicey personal behavior, had draped himself—rather than in boots and a cowboy hat—in Dionysian drag: "He stood by the door, wearing a thick garland of ivy and violets, with masses of ribbons trailing over his head, and said: 'Good evening, gentlemen. Will you let someone who's drunk—very drunk—join your symposium?'" (Gill translation).

In the ensuing bit of role reversal, Alcibiades, in his mid-thirties—about the same age as the host, Agathon, and Agathon's lover, Pausanias—tried to seduce Socrates, who was portrayed by sculptors at the time as a wizened satyr, like an old leather daddy But no such luck. Alcibiades even made a toast in praise of Socrates like those made earlier to the god Eros. Yet instead of succumbing, Socrates used the occasion to teach him a lesson.

"You must be seeing in me a beauty beyond comparison and one that's far superior to your own good looks," said Socrates. "If you've seen this and are trying to strike a deal with me in which we exchange one type of beauty for another, you're planning to make a good profit from me."

Socrates' punch line: "The mind's sight begins to see sharply when eyesight declines."

That night Alcibiades did get to fall asleep in the arms of Socrates. But nothing happened. Instead, Socrates stayed up debating tragedy versus comedy with Agathon until dawn. When the sun rose, he went off trailed by his devoted student Aristodemus, who mimicked his hero by going barefoot as well. "Socrates went to the Lyceum," reported Plato, "had a wash, spent the rest of the day as he did at other times, and only then in the evening went home to bed." Presumably he spent the day doing philosophy with his young male disciples whose *eros,* or "desire," was for truth and wisdom rather than for the mere internship to intimacy of physical love.

Socrates wasn't just making this stuff up as he went along. His philosophy was an adaptation. In the mythological tales he'd grown up on, the connection between love and soul had already been established. Of all the celebrity names linked romantically to Eros in these tales, the most frequent paparazzi sightings were of Psyche, or Soul. As the reports went, Psyche's sisters were easily married, but her own intimidating beauty kept most boys away. So her father consulted an oracle, who advised her to lie in a white wedding dress exposed on a rock until a horrible monster came to take possession.

This horrible monster turned out to be Eros, who came to lie beside her. (Those who'd been agitated by his presence were obviously out to destroy his reputation.) But Psyche accidentally spilled a drop of hot lamp oil on him by mistake, and he fled. Coached by Aphrodite, she then searched for Eros high and low, as low as the underworld—that is, love put her through hell. One moonlit eve, Eros finally rediscovered Psyche, his sleeping beauty, and awoke her by shooting into her one of his arousing arrows. The moral of the story: love and soul need each other.

When I wrote *Finding the Boyfriend Within*, I described the elusive Boyfriend Within, which the book was to be a helpful guide in discovering, as made up of our own best qualities. These admirable inner qualities might also be thought of as "that beauty itself" described by Socrates. I adapted this core concept to the dynamics of dating and social life at the workshop at Esalen by having everyone team up with a partner and after five or ten minutes of conversation describe the Boyfriend Within of their partner. My own partner was an actor from Canada whom I hadn't particularly noted in the group. Yet after speaking with him, seeking his Boyfriend Within, his own best qualities or inner beauty, I found myself confronted with a sort of knight encased in the shining armor of his own engaging personality.

EROTIC EXERCISE #5

While talking with someone you're interested in—on a date, at a bar, in the locker room—try to detect his finest inner qualities. You may think of these qualities as his Boyfriend Within, or inner beauty, or even soul. You can do this exercise in tandem with someone as an erotic game, or you can simply let it be your own secret.

By practicing looking for the "beauty itself" of a friendly face, you get to see Socrates' Eros in action. Rather than being a hindrance, the tickle of romantic or sexual interest actually stimulates perception. The experience may well be of someone transforming in front of your eyes. By looking for beauty, you often find beauty. The transformation you feel within could be a result of the openness and vulnerability required to perform this exercise successfully. If you're convinced that what you're seeing is deeper, or more loving, then you've proven Socrates right: there's more there than meets the eye.

A DATE WITH EROS

To go on a date with Eros means to go on a date that has some heart: not sentimental heart, but heart grounded in erotic attraction, though not necessarily of the Dionysian late-night variety. You could go on a Dionysian date with a porn star. But a date with Eros works better for either Valentine's Day excitement, the first red blush of romance, or to keep a spark going in an ongoing erotic friendship ("fuck buddies" is a favorite term for these), or for lovers in need of a fluff.

For my own erotic double, I chose Chris, a musician, but also a longtime on-again, off-again romantic interest. I first met Chris when he was twenty-one and I was thirty-six. (The age gap made us particularly suitable for a platonic setup.) At first, we—or I, at least—were entirely at the mercy of Eros number two, the romantic terrorist. I wrote bluesy poems where I was cast as the victim of love, suffering from what Diana Ross called a "love hangover." One gushing line from a sequence of sonnets I wrote for him during his younger, go-go dancer years: "I am in love with your pink shorts with flowers."

Several revolutions of the earth around the sun later, Chris and I are much more relaxed. Though we're hardly a couple, we exhibit some of the dynamics of commitment. Tenseness has given way to joking, sexual teasing to mental teasing. When we discussed our semiregular Saturday-night date, we made some ambitious plans: dancing at the Roxy, going to the Eagle. But when the evening arrived, the drag of the workweek limited us to dinner at a restaurant and a walk in the neighborhood, with the bonus of being able to come back to surf TV.

An African-American man, Chris, who at six feet two rises above me by a few inches, is covered in a skein of dark blue tattoos that barely show up on his skin. That night he was wearing blue jeans and a white V-neck T-shirt illustrated with a Buddha encircled in stars and resting in lotus position on the caption ZEN MECHANICS.

On the way to the restaurant, I kidded him about his tattoos.

"They're redundant, it's like black-on-black," I joked. "And what's the pentagram all about?"

"Pentagrams are greatly misunderstood," he began.

"Well, yes, and if you had a tattoo of a swastika you could say they're misunderstood, too. They're ancient Indian Sanskrit symbols imported by the Aryan invaders, but . . ."

In the red leather booth we requested at the restaurant, we ordered hamburgers and discussed the politics of the Middle East. Walking back home after dinner, we window-shopped at the Keith Haring boutique. Chris filled me in on the design of the dressing rooms at the new Prada store. We marveled at a Pakistani wedding party taking place in a street-level ballroom. The Doors' CD being played at a café where we stopped for mocha cappuccinos seemed unexpected but right.

"You're good on a date, you put out," I told him.

"Yeah . . . make them want more."

Digital TV is a fine erotic date tactic, if tactics are needed. You can actually get physical on a couch in a way prevented by stadium seating in a movie theater. And your partner will reveal his likes and dislikes invariably in the long menu of choices in the upper left corner of the screen. Chris and I had recently intersected in a passion for seventies movies. Last time it was *Looking for Mr. Goodbar,* this time *The Exorcist.* He'd seen both, I neither. On our list for the near future: *Cruising.*

One wall of my living room is lined with mirrors, another retro touch, I suppose. I remember round about midnight staring into the reflection of Chris, standing, half posing in a pair of white BVDs, yakking about something or other. (Chris talks a lot, sometimes at high volume.) But I was looking more *into* him at that point than at him. Sure, I was attracted to the shape of his tailored body, his cropped hair. But I could see in the quick succession of images, which he was stream-feeding to the mirror, different stages of his life—boy, young dude, current man, and then older Bill Cosby.

I saw into the black diamond of Chris's intelligent core in a facet of a moment, and in seeing, felt the powerful, magnetic presence of Eros. The arrows passed through my eyes and lit up my heart.

The possessed girl, Regan, in the movie having been exorcised of her demon, Chris and I eventually went to bed together around 2 A.M. with no questions asked. We had decided to have a sleepover. More like two guys in separate sleeping bags than passionate lovers, we quickly passed over into deep sleep. Only old friends could be so subliminally comfortable with each other.

The next day I was psyched that Chris decided to leave his Zen T-shirt. I wanted the novelty item for my collection. But when he exchanged it for one of my own heartfelt favorites, a clean Van Morrison antique T-shirt, I felt a sharp pain. Erotic dates are all about exchanges, some of which carry a bittersweet pang.

"I'll call you this week, I entered your number in my cell phone," Chris joked, parodying first-date dialogue as he passed through the blue velvet curtain and rumbled down the wooden steps from my top-floor apartment.

I didn't stall Chris's departure by telling him what I was really thinking—that in one night I had managed to experience with him all three of the main manifestations of Eros: the undiscriminating enthusiasm of our aimless, attentive walk as material boys through SoHo; the sexy, soft-porn titillation of a massage in front of a wall of mirrors; and finally, the glimpsing, by a ray of psychic light, of the heart of the matter, the essence of Chris—persisting through all the stages of his life from boy to man—which Socrates called "true beauty."

EROTIC EXERCISES

1. Close your eyes. Take a deep breath. Concentrate on the feeling in your heart, without any thought or words and without following any impulse to act.

2. Write a catalogue poem with "I love . . ." at the top of the page and your list of choices beneath.

3. List your teenage crushes.

4. List your current crushes. If you draw a blank, you can include crushes from movies, sports, or TV.

5. While talking with someone you're interested in— on a date, at a bar, in the locker room—try to detect his finest inner qualities. You may think of these qualities as his Boyfriend Within or inner beauty or even soul.

Six

ZEUS
THE GOD OF POWER

PROFILE

Zeus became the supreme god of gods—the *über*-god—the old-fashioned way: he earned it. Actually, he earned it the *really* old-fashioned way, by killing his father without a twinge of guilt. But then, he had a genetic predisposition to patricide. His grandfather Uranus kept all of his sons locked underground until Cronus, Zeus's father, cut off Uranus's cock and balls and splattered them across the sea. Fearing the same treatment, Cronus swallowed his sons at birth, except Zeus, whom he mistook for a stone. So Zeus started out as a kind of Che Guevara, a rebel with a cause, overthrowing his father's Titans by dint of new technology, the thunderbolt.

Then Zeus rose to the shaky position of Big Daddy. His regime change, however, was stable and progressive. Zeus brought some clarity to fatherhood. Presiding from the highest altitudes over the celestial manifestations of rain, thunder, and lightning, he became a sky god, enthroned on the craggy heights of Mount Olympus. As king not only of gods and weather but of men, he took responsibility (and Zeus *always* takes responsibility) for order and justice in the world. His responsibilities included purifying murderers of the stain of blood, ensuring that oaths were kept, and seeing that hospitality was extended by hosts to guests. All of human society was organized on a flow chart by eagle-eyed Zeus—the soaring, majestic bird being his emblem.

Of Zeus's many roles, father remains number one. Even the gods who were not his biological children addressed him as "Father," and all the gods rose when he walked into a clouded room. When immortalized in marble, he's always pictured as a mensch, with a curling beard and mustache, rocky forehead, and a weight lifter's body. Zeus shows awareness of the ultimate power and authority of his position in the *Iliad*, where he bluntly reminds those gathered for a board meeting of the pantheon: "So much stronger am I than the gods, and so much stronger than mortals." He is the CEO, chairman of the board, and majority stockholder of the Olympian franchise, the mogul of the entire universe.

Like many CEOs, Zeus was capable of the abuse of power. Though *Ktesios,* Protector of Property, he had his own boundary issues. Zeus was a compulsive quick-change artist, especially when trying to get in good with a desirable creature. He even turned himself into a snake to rape Rhea, his mother. Dubious qualities among the divine beings can have a silver lining: Zeus's skill at metamorphosis could be telling us that in supreme flexibility lies supreme power. Yet any sponsor of a Sexual Compulsives Anonymous group would detect an obvious pattern here, and Al-Anon might do well to recruit his ever-jealous wife, Hera, for her codependency. To seduce Leda, Zeus became a swan; to Danaë, he appeared as a golden shower; for Europa, he was a (most satisfying) bull.

In his few gay affairs, Zeus was always a top. While he had a brief affair with a childhood playmate, Aetos, his main love was Ganymede, the yellow-haired prince of Troy, the most beautiful of mortals. Ganymede's name in ancient Greek meant "delighting in genitals." In Latin, he became Catamitus, from which came "catamite," an English term for the passive partner in male intercourse. Zeus was the unqualified aggressor in this affair, first spotting Ganymede herding sheep on Mount Ida and sweeping down in the form of an eagle to whisk him away. Operating as a john, he then cut a deal: to the father, King Tros, he awarded "high-stepping horses." Ganymede was set up with the gift that keeps on giving, far outvaluing any number of condos, convertibles, or Hugo Boss suits—immortality.

Inexhaustible in sexual politics, Zeus was equally focused on the serious business of geopolitics. Outside the gates of his palace were two jars, one containing the white powder of good, the other the black powder of evil. He mixed these ingredients in different proportions to determine the fate of individuals, cities, and nations. In recognition of his role as a hands-on force in the politics of life, and as *Polieus,* God of Cities, the most massive of temples were those built in his honor in all cities, including Athens. The festival dedicated to Zeus at Olympia included all Greeks—and eventually even Macedonians and Romans—in the ceremony of lighting the Olympic torch and the running of the *stadion* race. Zeus was an unparalleled visionary, and this pan-Hellenic event was the United Nations General Assembly of the ancient world.

When the ancient Greeks wanted to think the biggest thought of which they were capable, they thought "Zeus." He expanded, for some, like a nitrous gas, until he became identical with everything that ever was or ever would be. This universal feeling was expressed in one of the Orphic hymns to Zeus:

> *Zeus is the first, Zeus is the last, the god with the*
> *dazzling lightning. . . . Zeus is the foundation of the*
> *earth and of the starry sky.*
>
> (KERENYI TRANSLATION)

In the Stoic school of philosophy, Zeus became the symbol of a single god, the incarnation of the cosmos. The laws of the world were considered nothing but his thoughts, and he became indistinguishable from Yahweh, God, or later, Allah, of the monotheistic religions.

But Homer didn't see it that way. And neither did most ancient Greeks. For them, Zeus remained the capo, the godfather of an extended family of gods and humans. His main contribution to Olympian spirituality was proactive power. He provided the infrastructure of the Olympian body. On his watch, the boundaries of freedom and responsibility were pushed. Aeschylus applauds this ambition in *Agamemnon:* "Whoever celebrates Zeus in the victory cry shall hit on sense entirely." But the code of Greek mythology stresses that he first needed to overcome the demons of his past, and to confront the authority of his own father, before clearing the way for cosmic evolution. Zeus's message to us: *Be your own daddy!*

MEDITATIONS AND EXERCISES

EMPOWERMENT

When I walked into my gym not long ago, I was faced with Silvano, a muscular Italian in his late thirties, who's been going through a life change as a trainer in training as well as a student returning to law school after a long hiatus. He made a snipping motion with his fingers, referring to my new haircut.

"You look eighteen," he said.

"You look eighty-one," I answered.

Silvano's face fell. I had to stop to explain that I was referring to his recent makeover, his allowing his black hair to tumble down to his shoulders and the growth of a thick beard flecked with silver. Together with the pumping up of his body, since he was now a walking advertisement for his own bodybuilding services, he looked positively Zeusian. When I invoked the god to explain my backward compliment, he approved, greatly lightening up.

"No, no . . . You look like Zeus, or at least Hercules."

"Oh, you mean like, 'Who's your daddy?'"

"Exactly."

In the think tank of the locker room, I was soon turning over in my mind his last comment. "Who's your daddy?". . . Hmm. "Who's your daddy?" is sex talk, a phrase lifted from the sex kittens of heterosexual porn by gay men and applied to their own issues of top or bottom, older or younger, provider or receiver. If you strip away all the innuendo and the imagery of *Deliverance*-style men in army fatigues, construction boots, with sprouts of chest hair flashing from their open flannel shirts, you are left not with a rhetorical question but with a basic question of identity.

In order to be truly empowered, we need to get to the bottom of the feelings we have about fathers. In that sense, we need to find out who *is* our daddy. It's a question that swirls through much ancient Greek literature, just as much as through contemporary sexual innuendo. When Athena, in the form of an army buddy, appears to Odysseus's son, Telemachus, to try to jazz him to set out to find his missing father, his answer is worthy of the "Deep Thoughts" segment of *Saturday Night Live*, though obviously pre–DNA testing:

> *My mother says indeed I am his. I for my part*
> *Do not know. Nobody really knows his own father.*
>   (LATTIMORE TRANSLATION)

Growing up in America, sons are more likely to bond—or pointedly not bond—with their dads on sports fields or at football stadiums than on battlefields. Billy Crystal outdid himself in reaching for a fly ball of a definition on Ken Burns's documentary *Baseball* when he recalled going to his first baseball games as a kid. "It's the wonder of holding your dad's hand," he said, "walking through that dark tunnel, and seeing the huge open space where men play the little boys' game." Don King flattened the sentiment a bit when he maladroitly tried to characterize his bond with superlightweight champion Julio Cesar Chavez: "We have a marriage, like a father and son."

Gays tend to have a more complicated relationship with sports and with their fathers. Part of the generational drama acted out at soccer games or Little League baseball parks is the son being imprinted with the father, replicating the behavior of the male role model. Researching an article a few years ago on men and sports for *Out* magazine, I was struck by the split-screen response to this tradition of "Gimme the ball" among gay youth. My friend Jeff, who played on his Dartmouth hockey and lacrosse teams, told me of his natural easing into the family jersey: "When I was growing up, the TV was always tuned to sports, sports, sports. I found it very exciting. The question was never whether I would pick up a hockey stick. It was just more like, 'Here's the hockey stick.'"

Not all transfers of power are so smooth or uniform. Jeff's friend John earned four varsity letters in swimming and football at the Army and Navy Academy in Carlsbad, California, as well as a soccer scholarship. Yet his pileup of citations didn't solve his oedipal conflicts: "I was under a lot of pressure to perform when I was a kid. My father one day took me to the Little League tryouts. He didn't even ask me if I wanted to, he just said, 'Come on, we're going.' A lot of it was for my father. I wanted his love and approval, but I never got it. So in a way the whole thing was a big waste of time."

An NYU English professor shared a curious reversal with me of this setup from the father's point of view. A Shakespearean scholar, he never had any interest in sports until his son turned out to be an avid baseball player and pitcher for New York's Stuyvesant High School team. As his open-faced son told me, "It feels good to be part of something. People who aren't on a team are definitely missing an experience." The professor felt responsible in his role as good dad to attend his son's games, where he'd position himself down at the fence, rooting along with all the other fathers. Yet he'd feel intimidated, as well, because he couldn't yell out any advice as he didn't entirely understand the game.

"You know how Freud talks about young men needing the approval of their fathers," said a gay New Jersey high school basketball coach. "A lot of young boys who excel on the sports field achieve instant acceptance from their fathers. A lot of gays don't get acceptance from their fathers . . . because they don't share sports as a bond. Also, a lot of gays don't experience bonding with other boys. I think that's why a lot of healthy-minded gay guys I've known have had lots of friends. They don't go out to the bars alone. There's camaraderie there." Not only is the child the father to the man but, according to the coach, the man is often forever the child of the father.

To have some freedom—the ultimate Zeusian value—in our relations with the fatherly part of ourselves, we need to begin with our real-life father, or whoever was the closest approximation. A successful actress once told me that her best weapon was kindness. In sports terms, her remark could be translated as, "The best offense is a good defense." She said that if someone attacked her, in person or in print, she was doubly nice when she saw them socially. Her attitude deflected, diffused, or even defeated them more than any tit-for-tat exchange she might concoct. Zeus used a thunderbolt to resolve his issues with his father. But his Titan-age rebellion took place eons ago. We're likely to get further with the tactic of killing kindness, used by my actress friend, to approach our fathers, or the memory or mental image of our fathers, positively rather than negatively.

ZEUSIAN EXERCISE #1

List happy memories of your father.

My list included

- His gift of a red toy car brought home to me from a business trip
- Watching him make a home run in a chamber of commerce ball game
- Saturday afternoon father-son dates at matinees of sci-fi movies
- Nightly updates when my mother was in the hospital

Contrary to the line immortalized by Janis Joplin, "Freedom's just another word for nothing left to lose," Zeusian freedom is about there being much to gain. The expression of that freedom is choice. We might not have the freedom to choose our family, race, or genetic code. They are part of our destiny. Even Zeus didn't have final power over *moira,* destiny, which Greek mythology pictured as his three daughters, like backup singers, who spun, wound up, and then snipped the thread of each individual's life. But we do have the power to choose our attitude to these givens.

We also have the power to add cards to the deck we've been dealt. Father figures are just such cards. These are fathers we've chosen for ourselves along the way. Usually they are older men in positions of authority, or relatives who possess a quality we find attractive. Our own instincts or needs will naturally lead us to these men. As we start filling in the crossword puzzle of our identity, the names of these men spell themselves out. We usually recognize their significance only in retrospect, when their true importance becomes felt in later life. In identifying them, we gain important self-knowledge. They represent aspects of ourselves we were trying to actualize, or to father.

ZEUSIAN EXERCISE #2

List father figures you've gravitated toward in your life. Next to each name, write the main quality they represent to you.

My list of father figures:

- Reverend Miller: religion
- Debbie's dad: books
- Kenneth Koch: poetry

When I was twelve, I began dragging my mother to church because of a fascination I developed with a local Presbyterian minister, who then baptized me. Only years later, I realized that the slick gentleman in the black Thunderbird that was idling in front of the church as we exited each Sunday was the minister's boyfriend. Puberty and spiritual curiosity were combined for me in the figure of Reverend Miller. Debbie was my high school girlfriend, but I wonder if I didn't spend more time at her house to be with her father, a world traveler who worked for the Red Cross and talked with me about his vast library. Kenneth Koch encouraged me in writing poetry while I was a student in his creative writing seminar at Columbia College. He made incisive comments (like those of the teacher of Japanese brush painting). I recall him saying once to my puzzled nineteen-year-old self: "You rely too much on authority."

Similar to a father figure, but ultimately depleting rather than empowering if relied on to excess, is the sugar daddy. I suppose Kenneth Koch was saying, in a sense, "Beware sugar daddies!" In the rites of passage of gay life, sugar daddies have their role. These are older men who support younger men, usually financially. We all have a Ganymede aspect to ourselves—the young boy who can't resist being swept off his feet by a big, strong eagle and taken to live rent-free in a brass palace on Mount Olympus. This ritual is acted out nightly in hustler bars with names like Rent Boys or Tricks. But you don't need to push all the way to the margins of male prostitution to find the Zeus-Ganymede dynamic. Youth and beauty are often exchanged for money and power in more ordinary ways—dinners at restaurants topping the Zagat guide's recommended list; Italian suits from Barneys; a weekend on South Beach. To quote the exhilarating chorus of "Sugar Daddy" from *Hedwig and the Angry Inch:* "If you've got some sugar for me, / Sugar daddy, bring it home."

Sexual positions and finances aside, though, the Ganymede experience truly pays off only when integrated with the Zeus experience. Unless you have it in writing, intercession from above might never arrive. Ganymede scored the gift of immortality. But for mortals, Zeus's defining quality of individual responsibility needs to be awakened in a timely fashion. In Tennessee

Williams's *A Streetcar Named Desire,* Blanche Dubois delivers her famous parting line, "I have always depended on the kindness of strangers." The irony of her farewell, of course: she is about to be carted off to a mental institution.

ZEUSIAN EXERCISE #3

List the areas in your life where you feel deprived, or where you wish someone would intervene to help. These areas of need might be mental, emotional, physical, or financial.

My wish list included

- Condo
- Beach house
- A Jag

In *Finding the Boyfriend Within,* I addressed the issue of wishing that a Zeus or a Ganymede would suddenly appear to fill an emotional need. Either because self-nurturing plus a healthy dating life works, or because I've grown more superficial, my wish list was now definitely financially rather than emotionally skewed. A short-term solution I found: spend money—consciously buy gifts for myself or others as a reminder of how much of a providing Zeus I already am. A midrange solution: read helpful books on financial planning, such as Andrew Tobias's *The Only Investment Guide You'll Ever Need.* A long-term solution: generate work projects. My message to myself hasn't just been *Be your own daddy,* but specifically, *Be your own sugar daddy!*

THE POWER OF EDUCATION

Some Greek gods are associated more than others with one stage of life. Hephaestus evokes the pangs of adolescence, the bittersweet pains that accompany first love and the composition of first poems or songs. Though creativity is a lifelong gift, Hephaestus is the deity of what Kurt Cobain called "teen spirit." Dionysus is another god for the readers of *Spin* magazine. Zeus is definitely an adult deity. While issues of power and responsibility are ageless, his prime time remains middle age. His subscription base is more likely that of the *Economist* or *American Educator.*

When I turned forty, I finally got a steady job as a professor at a state university in New Jersey. I'd been working as a freelance journalist for ten years, writing mostly as a hired gun for glossy fashion magazines. Yet I always felt in free fall. I sometimes worried that I was being paid to simulate a house voice whose corporate opinions were not always mine. A less high-minded concern: I wanted health insurance and a retirement plan. A former professor alerted me to a creative-writing tenure-track line being advertised, and I went for it.

My first few months on the job, I suffered through an identity crisis. A Manhattanite who had not yet discovered the magic of the automobile, I took the bus three mornings a week from Port Authority. Riding in boxy public transport, staring at the ruins of the industrial age through its gray-tinted windows, I worried about my decision. My resolve wavered. I wondered whether I should pitch a story on the new Calvin Klein underwear model and return to my beat. I grew curious about who was lining the runways of the Helmut Lang show this season.

The unconvincing red-and-blue diagonally striped old school tie around my neck was chafing.

By spring semester, I'd come around. Looking back, the downshift in gears turned out to have been the best of all possible life moves. Monday mornings helped. I was always astonished on my weekly return to campus at the physical appearance of teenagers—I hadn't been exposed to the latest model of recent high school grad in my life in Manhattan. "Their skin is literally pink"—I remember telephoning a friend with my discovery. As many of the male undergrads dressed the same as gay men—a style borrowed from the homoerotic fashion ads photographed by Bruce Weber—I had to stop myself from cruising. I was confused by all the Abercrombie & Fitch T-shirts, Nike sneakers, and baseball caps swiveled backward.

The biggest boon of my new occupation proved to be spiritual. I found an opportunity for expressing a male nurturing aspect I'd never known I had. By exercising the qualities of teaching, helping, advising, giving, and becoming a sort of academic coach figure, I underwent a transformation. Surprisingly asked by the most notorious football fraternity to be their sponsor, I was breathing the freedom of being positioned on an appropriate ordinate on my life curve. Such adjusting to the continuous process of maturation was central to Carl Jung's notion of psychological health. As he wrote, with a wink at Dionysus, "The wine of youth does not always clear with advancing years; sometimes it grows turbid." Teaching helped to clarify my wine.

An article in the *New York Times* on the arrival of Cornel West as a professor at Princeton one fall semester stressed the effect of the transfer of power through education from the other side: the side of the students. In an introductory freshman class in which he was teaching Plato's *Republic,* West remarked that Socrates had decided to leave his father's craft of stonemasonry to become "a sculptor of men and women." After the class, a seminar student told the reporter, "I can imagine that Socrates' disciples were as taken with him as we are with Professor West. While Professor West mentioned the molding of individuals and fostering of original ideas, I also thought of how every one of us in the class probably is just waiting to offer something special to the rest of the world and that Professor West is the very means to that."

Education has power no matter which role you're in, or what is being studied or taught. Education can give practical tools—like going to air conditioner maintenance school or taking a driving class. The gossip columnist William Norwich wrote an entire, whimsical novel, *Learning to Drive,* from just such a midlife education. But one of the pleasures of education as an adult can be the impracticality of what is being studied. I took an introductory class in Arabic for two semesters, and the teacher adopted a grade school presence to make a difficult subject seem lighter. (The class would clap if anyone actually got the pronunciation down.) The fun is always somewhat serious, though; the evidence of Zeus's presence is the rush of power that accompanies almost any kind of learning. As the poet Yeats asks in his poem about Zeus's rape of Leda, "Leda and the Swan": "Did she put on his knowledge with his power?"

ZEUSIAN EXERCISE #4

Enroll in a class to learn a skill or to study a subject that piques your curiosity, or consider joining a peer learning group.

137

Possibilities include

- A foreign language class
- A computer class
- A reading group at a bookstore or library
- Flying lessons for piloting a small plane
- Returning to school to complete an undergrad or graduate degree

To become a true daddy, you must eventually not only empower yourself but learn to nurture others. Every daddy, by definition, has what income tax forms define as dependents. Even those who don't have children of their own have the possibility to fulfill the role of mentor, big brother, godparent, uncle, or teacher. Filling such a role isn't selfless. The boy or girl, nephew or niece you take under your aegis, or shield, won't be the only beneficiary. To go through life without experiencing the joy of educating and nurturing is to sustain a loss.

ZEUSIAN EXERCISE #5

Engage in a mentoring or nurturing activity.

Some options for being someone else's daddy:

- Coaching a sports team
- Volunteering in a nondiscriminatory big brothers program
- Spending quality time with a niece or nephew, goddaughter or godson
- Tutoring

A DATE WITH ZEUS

For a date with Zeus, choose an activity that tampers with power—personal, educational, political, or all three.

Henry David Thoreau warned, "Beware of all enterprises that require new clothes." But when entering into the realms of Zeus, you often need to suit up. My choice for a Zeusian date was to accept an invitation to a benefit evening entitled "Come Write History," dedicated to gay and lesbian literature. Each of us writers was the host for a table of ten guests. The money raised was intended to be used for political action in support of gay issues. When I accepted, the organizer of the event called to clue me in: "You should wear a suit or a blazer, and a tie. It's business attire."

On the assigned evening, I showed up in my gray suit at the New-York Historical Society for a warm-up cocktail party, which began at seven. Crowded into a hallway lined with paintings of the Hudson River School, as waiters circulated with trays of sushi hors d'oeuvres and clinking glasses of drinks, the guests made small talk with one another and with a procession of politicians who apparently wished to curry favor with gay voters and opinion makers. I spoke for a bit with a former vice president of the United States and then with a candidate running for governor of New York state.

At eight o'clock we were ushered into the main banquet hall. The "real" politicians and their spouses made their exits. But then their engagement in the hallway, squeezing hands and smiling in a fixed way without much eye contact, seemed like a mastery of the mannerism more than the substance. I sensed in the authors, guests, and more committed politicians finding their way to their name cards a more palpable politics of the style that occurs face-to-face. My guest was Eric, my computer geek friend, who now had more time as he'd extricated himself from his burgeoning relationship. Tall and wiry, with John Lennon eyeglasses, Eric looked discontinuous with his blue suit: like a scarecrow in blue serge.

I had never been a gung ho political activist. But looking over at the next table at Edmund White, the author of *A Boy's Own Story,* I flashed back about twenty-five years to one of the earliest gay pride marches down Fifth Avenue in Manhattan. We'd both been in the writers' contingent—in those days, writing and taking photographs about our lives *was* politics. Our scraggly corps held up placards celebrating famous gay and lesbian writers, such as Rimbaud, Whitman, and Virginia Woolf, with drawn caricatures of our heroes like those now on bookstore shopping bags. When we reached the New York Public Library, we scampered up its imposing steps and posed there for no one in particular.

The official speakers of this evening were political mostly by dint of having written essays and novels bound for the time capsule of history. Edward Albee defended Susan Sontag, recently excoriated for her op-ed opinions on the semantics of terms such as "cowardice" and "war." E. Lynn Harris recalled the local politics of losing his high school election because of a vote count problem. Charles Kaiser boomed without even a mike— he'd been singularly responsible as a young reporter for hectoring the *Times* into finally using the word "gay." A young novelist, Alex Sanchez, read e-mails from high school students. Ann Bannon, the queen of lesbian pulp fiction, took a bow as the lurid covers of her novels from the fifties were held up. Patricia Nell Warren (*The Front Runner*) talked of "writing our history, then and now."

At least as much of a rush came from the table talk, between courses of crabmeat salad and sea bass, among politically engaged guests who removed the towering Plexiglas centerpiece and flowers to ease our conversation. "Maybe the government knows something we don't," one was saying. "Then why don't they give that information to Germany, or Japan?" "I'm opposed to using the phrase 'axis of evil' when referring to Americans; the greatest danger is to turn on ourselves," worried another about a zinger in one of the speeches. "Hitler should be ruled out as a comparison. Isn't there a statute of limitations on his name? As soon as someone uses that example, all the lights of reason go off."

"Wow, I don't think I've ever been at a table of gay guys quite like this," Eric whispered to me, impressed. "Everyone's so smart, so current, so informed . . . No one's talking about Gucci."

After a dessert of chocolate pyramids with ginger and quince and two hours of thought, words, and plans for action, we were finished. Among this working crowd, which included lots of investment bankers and corporate lawyers, eleven o'clock was the cutoff. Books were still being autographed by and for authors as Eric and I made our way toward the archway of an exit door. The chairman was announcing that three quarters of a million dollars had been raised, and there was more applause.

Standing just outside the doorway was the author Rita Mae Brown, ruddy-faced, dressed in a white button-down shirt. I eavesdropped as a young man, probably in his late thirties, went up to her as a fan, revealing the mysterious manner in which

literature, education, and politics can impact lives in an un-
intended fashion. "I just wanted to thank you," he said. "*Ruby-
fruit Jungle* was *my* coming-out book. Even if it was about
lesbians, it was the first gay book I ever read. It encouraged me."

As we descended the unfurling scroll of steps out into the
rain, Eric, in his understated monotone, made a comment that
speared the essence of the Zeusian dynamic of the evening:
"There were lots of sugar daddies in there."

ZEUSIAN EXERCISES

1. Write down a list of happy memories of your father.

2. List father figures you've gravitated toward in your life. Next to each name, write the main quality that person represents to you.

3. List areas in your life where you feel deprived, or where you wish someone would intervene to help you.

4. Enroll in a class to learn a skill or to study a subject that piques your curiosity, or consider joining a peer learning group.

5. Engage in a mentoring or nurturing activity.

Seven

THE INNER ORACLE OF SOCRATES

PROFILE

Whent Plato was a twenty-something young man, he had trouble deciding what he wanted to be when he grew up. The son of a rich, political family, he knocked around Athens trying on different lifestyles. For a while he was an amateur wrestler. Born Aristocles, "Plato" was actually his stage name, meaning "broad," for his beefy shoulders. Twice Plato carried off the wrestling prize at the Isthmian Games, but he never made it to the big time of the Olympics. Next he decided to be a great poet, but just didn't have the tragic touch to impress the judges in any of the major competitions. Having failed to bring home the gold, he had resigned himself to cashing in on his pedigree by running for public office.

Then he met the sixty-something philosopher Socrates, and as one scholar has written, "It was love at first sight." Socrates had that effect on people. By the time they met, Socrates had

145

long ago given up his day job as stonemason and sculptor to spend all his time in the public square asking probing questions about life and death of his circle of young disciples. A self-professed "philosopher"—lover of wisdom—he was a devotee of Apollo. The feeling was apparently mutual. One of the most famous examples of buzz in the ancient world was the pronouncement of Apollo's oracle at Delphi that there was no man wiser than Socrates. Wittily, Socrates claimed to have earned the title "Wisest Man Alive" because "I neither know nor think that I know."

A crisis in the lives of Socrates, Plato, and the city of Athens was Socrates' trial in 399 B.C. Accused of not believing in the gods and of corrupting the young—Plato being a prime example—Socrates was sentenced to death by a vote of 280 to 220. At the center of the controversy was another of Socrates' young followers, Alcibiades, whose name always spelled trouble. Five years earlier, he'd been involved in a Spartan plot to overthrow Athenian democracy, and Socrates found himself swept up in the blame. When the hour came for Socrates to drink hemlock poison in his cell, he sent away his wife, Xanthippe, and two sons to prevent any melodrama, allowing only his male disciples to remain. Although Plato claimed to have been absent from the execution, the French neoclassical painter David in *The Death of Socrates* poses him at Socrates' feet, as the philosopher talks himself through his own death.

This placement is poetic justice, for Plato spent the rest of his life working on his masterwork, a literary docudrama of Socrates' life as a philosopher. Using lots of poetic license, Plato spliced together footage from his own head with other wishful scenes to create his dialogues, which were packaged as eyewitness accounts of the walks and talks of Socrates, who never wrote down a word while alive. The most dramatic is the *Apology*, which was Plato's remembered transcript of Socrates' closing argument at his trial. Socrates definitely didn't deliver a Johnnie Cochran–style, "If the glove doesn't fit, you must acquit" defense. Instead, he went public with his Inner Oracle. This admission might well have pushed a few undecided Athenian voters over the edge.

Actually the word Socrates used was *daimon*, which has since been translated as "inner oracle," "internal oracle," "inner voice," or "prophetic guide." A *daimon* in ancient Greek was basically any higher power or spirit. We can hear our own word "demon" in the ancient Greek, though its sinister, devilish aspect wasn't a given with the *daimones*. They stood in the middle, between gods and men. They were thought of as interpreters or ferrymen who communicated messages or gifts from men to gods and from gods to men, prayer and sacrifices from one side, commands and recompenses from the other. Plato used the word *daimones* for fallen war heroes as well. Socrates did his usual trick of taking something superstitious or religious and making of it a practical psychological component in the search for wisdom. He relocated the source of the spiritual or heroic within.

That Socrates was guided by his Inner Oracle was not news to Plato and company. They'd known for years. He never went into politics, thanks to his Inner Oracle. On his way to a cocktail party or the gym, he would often stop, pixilated by some thought process, which his young friends knew to be the Inner Oracle making its presence felt. One such moment occurred on his way to Agathon's dinner party, recorded in *The Symposium*.

Aristodemus, who'd been walking with Socrates until he dropped off, had to prevent the host from sending a servant out to find the missing guest as dinner was getting cold: "No, by all means leave him alone! He has a way of doing this. Sometimes he goes into a trance just where he happens to be standing. He'll come back presently, I know it. Don't move him—let him be!"

At his trial, Socrates laid it out for everybody—he possessed a divine spark of goodness and truth within that trumped anyone else's judgment: "You have heard me speak at sundry times and in divers places of an oracle or sign which comes to me. . . . This sign, which is a kind of voice, first began to come to me when I was a child." Socrates assumes that since he hadn't violated his consciousness of an Inner Oracle in anything he'd said or done at the trial, then death must be the final test of his integrity:

Hitherto the divine faculty of which the internal oracle is the source has constantly been in the habit of opposing me even about trifles, if I was going to make a slip or error in any matter; and now you see there has come upon me that which may be thought, and is generally believed to be, the last and worst evil. But the oracle made no sign of opposition, either when I was leaving my house in the morning, or when I was on my way to court, or while I was speaking, at anything which I was going to say; and yet I have often been stopped in the middle of a speech, but now in nothing I either said or did touching the matter at hand has the oracle opposed me.

(JAVETT TRANSLATION)

This single speech changed Plato's life and led to the creation of Western philosophy. Some have colored Socrates crazy. Certainly the Athenians did—if not crazy, dangerous. But his premise was simple: everyone has an inner voice full of personal wisdom. Socrates deduced that if he had such a voice, then everybody does. So he began talking with many of the young men of Athens to get to know their Inner Oracles more intimately. Through a game of twenty questions, known as the "Socratic method," he drew from them opinions on the big issues of life. What began as his own game of solitaire turned into a lively game of hearts that created enough of a stir that we're still getting a contact high from Socrates' conversations twenty-five centuries later.

Socrates was put to death for disrespecting the ancient Greek gods. Actually, he contributed the one crucial element lacking in the virtual body of the pantheon: soul. Without the soul of the Inner Oracle, these ancient deities would now be much less accessible. They would indeed be dead. With the Inner Oracle, they become animated for us. We can integrate their archetypal forces in our lives through our own Inner Oracle. Because of his discovery of this all-important divine faculty, Socrates—thanks to the love of Plato for his spiritual hero—still gets top billing among those who can change lives. As Andrew Harvey wrote in his anthology *Essential Gay Mystics*, "Socrates was the first avowedly homosexual 'mystic.'"

MEDITATIONS AND EXERCISES

THE SOCRATIC VOICE WITHIN

In Philip Pullman's trilogy for young adults, *His Dark Materials,* every character possesses a daemon. These accompanying guardian spirits take the shape of cats, terriers, moths, sparrows, even a golden monkey. The heroine, Lyra Belacqua, a precocious orphan growing up within the precincts of Oxford University, has a daemon, sometimes pictured as a dark brown moth, other times as a goldfinch or terrier, all named Pantalaimon. One peculiarity in these manifestations of the characters' souls in animal form is that they may shift shape during childhood, but through a process called "settling," adults finally possess a single, fixed daemon.

Lyra and a seaman with a seagull for his daemon discuss this situation as she's being borne—Harry Potter or Bilbo Baggins style—toward a terribly adult adventure in the cold far North:

"Why do daemons have to settle?" Lyra asked. "I want Pantalaimon to be able to change forever. So does he."

"Ah, they have always settled, and they always will. That's part of growing up. There'll come a time when you'll be tired of his changing about and you'll want a settled kind of form for him."

Pullman's daemons are fanciful, but they aren't so far off from Socrates'. His was obviously the inspiration—though without the innovation of the mutability of childhood daemons introduced by Pullman. We know of Socrates mostly because of the fame he gained for the conversational method he developed for doing philosophy, with his *daimon* being given less attention. But the back-and-forth of his all-important method might well have begun for him with his early childhood experience of an inner feeling expressed in an inner voice to which he learned to become attuned. In another of Plato's dialogues, *Gorgias*, he says as much when he compares himself to a musical instrument, either in or out of tune:

> I do believe that it would be better for me that my lyre or a chorus I directed should be out of tune and loud with discord, and that multitudes of men should disagree with me rather than that my single self should be out of harmony with myself and contradict me.
>
> (W. C. HEMBOLD TRANSLATION)

As I got to know my Boyfriend Within during the process I recorded in *Finding the Boyfriend Within*, I needed to wrap my head around some similar notions. Finding my Boyfriend Within was hardly a philosophical quest. Mostly I was just learning to date myself, and much of this process was taken up with making dinners for one or buying yellow roses. But the exercise with which I began the process, and which threads throughout the book, was the carrying on of an inner dialogue with my Voice Within. As I wrote then: "It was this Voice I 'heard' that led me to get more in touch with that part of myself I've come to think of as the Boyfriend Within." My well-meaning Boyfriend Within was perhaps not so far off from Socrates' *daimon*.

Recently someone said to me, "I had that book of yours for a while and never looked at it much . . . then I went through a weird period and suddenly it all made sense. I guess it's made for certain times of life . . . like, passages of life." Certainly the themes and exercises of the book spoke to me most intently at a certain time of my life. Now, I oscillate in and out—encounters such as that with Renaldo reminding me of its basic, necessary truths. But the single exercise that has become a daily habit ever since has been conversing with the Voice Within. Having conducted workshops and corresponded with readers over the years since its publication, I can vouch confidently that the exercise works universally for all those who approach their own inner voice openly and patiently.

While anyone can tap into their Voice Within and begin to gain the benefits of this customized, personal reorientation—couture rather than off-the-rack spirituality—not everyone can get started so easily. I discovered along the way that some people need to loosen up first, like weight lifters stretching at the gym or dancers limbering at a bar. A good equivalent to stretching is automatic writing. For those feeling awkward at an encounter of the first kind with their Voice Within, and for more advanced types as well, automatic writing is a helpful warm-up.

SOCRATIC EXERCISE #1

Practice automatic writing by putting down on paper whatever comes into your head without stopping or censoring yourself. Continue nonstop for at least five or ten minutes.

A couple of random lines of my own nonsense:

I feel like Forrest Gump I should be in pain but the sun is so
   beautiful
on the quilt rug the carpenters remind me of Milan taking the
   free buses
being so lonely the model who died all that beauty and lust and
   the isolation

Eventually after a few pages of such sputtering wishes, lies, and dreams, you may find yourself winding down to finding out what matters to you in the moment. Then you're ready for a conversation with the Voice Within.

Like someone on a first date, or in the heat of the first months of a romance, I was overly formal in my initial dealings with my Voice Within. "Fetishistic" and "obsessive-compulsive" were the put-downs used by some unimpressed friends who were reading the book. I may have emphasized too much the need to return to the same spot every day for this inner dialogue (in my case, a kitchen table) and to use two different colored pens to record "his" and "my" questions and answers—though such reinforcing practices are helpful for beginners. As I began to rely more on this process in everyday life, I found myself scratching dialogues with my inner voice on the back of envelopes or tapping them out on the keyboard of a laptop during a plane trip. So I dispensed with some of the procedure. My Voice Within and I are now much more like an old married couple: we don't dress for dinner.

What has remained essential is the dialogue format. I realize now that I intuitively mimicked the Socratic dialectical method when first approaching my Voice Within. The basic exercise of getting in touch with the Voice Within is: sit down; take a deep breath to clear the mind; write down a question about something that is bothering you, either trivial or important, and wait for an answer. Write down the answer.

Identify yourself by your initials, and your Voice Within by "VW." The details of transcribing aren't important. But as Socrates discovered, the truth-seeking mind works best by keeping the conversational form—as in one of Plato's dialogues.

SOCRATIC EXERCISE #2

Begin a daily practice of writing down a dialogue with your Voice Within.

Here's one of my daily dialogues. No concern is too trivial for the Voice Within.

BG: Do I want to chat online?

VW: I think you should take the day off from that.

BG: It's a waste of time?

VW: It's relaxing to waste time. You deserve to waste some time.

BG: Then why not?

VW: Today, when you think of chatting online, you feel a tightening in your heart. That's not good.

SOCRATIC VALUES

If no concern is too trivial for the Voice Within, neither is any concern too deep or philosophical. In Plato's *Republic,* Socrates defends his talk show of a life by explaining that his discussions were "not about any chance question, but about the way one should live." The Voice Within exercise initially lends itself to chance questions. In the process of becoming comfortable with my Boyfriend Within, much of my rambling inner dialogue pointed me toward leading a more comfortable life. But as the anxiety of boyfriend hunting was gradually displaced or peeled away like an onion skin, new, core questions about "the way one should live" revealed themselves, too.

On the road with the book in the past few years, I've found others who were becoming adept enough at their exercise with the Voice Within to begin asking bigger questions as well. "What are we having for dinner?" is a fine, immediate question for the Boyfriend Within, especially when coming to terms with living alone or even spending one or two nights happily alone rather than otherwise engaged. At the couple of workshops at Esalen, I began to experiment with groups of advanced practitioners in asking the Voice Within for answers to some of the sorts of questions about values that Socrates took on in the dialogues. Among the timeless questions that were raised by him in those early dialogues are, for instance: What's the difference between sexual love and friendship? Is knowledge the source of happiness? Is there a connection between a healthy body and a healthy soul?

I was amazed to find that everyone at the first workshop could discover his own mind on issues never before so directly confronted. Their answers often surprised even the questioner. As one participant said, "This isn't what I would have said off the top of my head if you'd asked me. The answers from my Voice Within sound more like tough love." This method of truth finding proved to be particularly gay-friendly because there's no top-down authority. As Mark Thompson, D.C., a chiropractor from San Francisco, contributed at a subsequent seminar, "I think that gay men have a special gift in being able to listen to 'that still small voice within.' I mean, we wouldn't be out if we hadn't paid attention to an inner voice prompting us to do something that was different from what everyone else was doing, and which can be pretty unpopular."

SOCRATIC EXERCISE #3

Use the Voice Within as an Inner Oracle to discover your answers to the basic philosophical and spiritual questions of life and to identify your values.

Some of my questions and answers, arranged according to Olympian principles and culled from rambling inner conversations that actually went on for pages:

Apollonian principle

    BG: What's wisdom?

    VW: Living attuned to me . . . your VW.

Dionysian principle

    BG: What's sex?

    VW: Sex enhances life. It's the sizzle on the steak.

    BG: Then why has sex been the ticket to so many self-destructive downers?

    VW: If you go for the sizzle without the steak, you wind up malnourished.

Hermeneutic principle

BG: What's social life all about?

VW: Transmitting messages. Wisdom comes as much from voices outside of you as from within . . . Don't stop going out.

Hephaestian principle

BG: What book should I write next?

VW: Keep going to Japanese brush painting class. The answer will come to you from painting, not from thinking.

Erotic principle

BG: What is romance?

VW: Romance comes from the heart. Like the mind, the heart can be tricky. But romance has its own reasons. Stay open to having the falling-in-love feeling as often as possible every day.

Zeusian principle

BG: What's the meaning of life?

VW: Could you rephrase that, please?

BG: OK. Where do I get my power?

VW: By doing something for someone else. Volunteer. Nurture others. Take responsibility. Give back. Be quiet about the good you do. The strongest power is invisible.

SOCRATIC DATES

A few years ago, a critic shot a barb at me across the bow of a Sacramento newspaper. Reviewing my advice book, she decided to dish out her own advice: "Were Brad to ask me how to get a boyfriend, I think I'd recommend he start by listening to others, listen to what they care about, what they're fearful of, what turns them on . . . and off, what their favorite color is, what they did in high school, and about their first time, and the worst time."

I saved her review because I thought she was dead-on, especially if her advice wasn't just telescoped for potential boyfriends but included all friends and acquaintances, and if the topics of discussion could be expanded beyond high school chapbook concerns to encompass the big issues of life and death. I know she was trying to get in a dig, basically saying, "Oh, just get a boyfriend and be done with it." But what I chose to take away was her finding of a connection between the Voice Within and others' voices, which was the next logical step, taken by Socrates himself in his spiritual quest.

A sort of money shot in the history of Western civilization was Socrates' own philosophical epiphany on this matter, which is entirely a matter of guesswork, of course. I like to imagine him at a symposium, which was basically a cocktail party, suddenly realizing that the voice of wisdom he heard within was also audible in others. At that moment, in my fantasy, he begins dating all the most intelligent and attractive young men of Athens. At least one intellectual fascinated by Socrates, Hannah Arendt, wrote about just such a connection between what Socrates did when alone with his *daimon* and his social life, which consisted of lots of *elenchos*, which is Hellenistic Greek for "inquiry" or "cross-examination." She wrote that Socrates "makes public in discourse the thinking process—the dialogue that goes on within me, between me and myself."

Christopher Phillips, a teacher and journalist from New Jersey, has begun trying to re-create this ancient dynamic in what he calls Socrates Cafés. A founder of the nonprofit Society for Philosophical Inquiry, he's been facilitating freelance, one-night-only encounters across the country at such equivalents to the ancient agora as coffee shops, senior centers, assisted-living complexes, prisons, libraries, day care centers, elementary and high schools, and churches. During his philosophical stand-up routines, which he's been presenting since 1997, he motivates those attending to pick a question and begin cross-examining one another on "Life's Big Questions," including the meaning of love, friendship, work, or growing old. The epigram to Phillips's book *Socrates Café: A Fresh Taste of Philosophy* is Socrates' favorite come-on line: "Can I ask you a question?"

What's missing in Phillips's noble project is perhaps only the erotic, which was an important ingredient in the original. One-on-one dating adds just that cinnamon to the cappuccino. Dating can be refreshed with the help of the god Hephaestus by going outside the cliché of the meeting at a coffee shop. But you can also refresh dating by going deeper. When you're sitting at that Starbucks table with your new, or old, friend, you just might introduce a Socratic tease into the conversation. Ask him: "Do you think sex and love can co-exist?" Or, "Do you believe in God?" You don't have to overdo it. But there will likely be some frisson after such a question. You can also invent an online screen name or profile to attract such dialogue and such interlocutors. By using the temporary screen name SpiritualDude for a few months, I had many Socratic exchanges of instant messages and e-mails. *Elenchos* can turn out to be just the nip that turns a random encounter into a soulful exchange. As such legendary pairs as Abelard and Héloïse or Rumi and Shams teach us by example, few things are more romantic than soulful.

SOCRATIC EXERCISE #4

Go on a date devoted to talking about life's big issues with an acquaintance, friend, or lover. Or insinuate a few moments of Socratic cross-examination into an ordinary conversation or online encounter.

By expanding the concept of a date to include any meeting at which a meaningful dialogue transpires, you may discover your date book filling up quickly. After giving a talk in the basement of an Episcopal church in Maplewood, New Jersey, I found myself on a train back to Manhattan with a young man who'd been sitting in the front row. He turned out to be an investment banker from Brooklyn. Our conversation definitely fulfilled the requirements for a Socratic date.

Here is an outtake, which, of course, is not literally accurate, but is *at least* as reliable as Plato's renditions of Socrates' conversations, written down sometimes decades after the event. I am BG, the investment banker is IB.

IB: I definitely feel that gays are on the verge of a spiritual awakening.

BG: I wouldn't argue with you there.

IB: From a marketing point of view, the brand needs to be refreshed.

BG: (*laughing*) I've felt that for a while. But it's a different kind of spirituality. You can't leave out sex this time. Gay guys aren't going to crusade for celibacy.

IB: I know my partner and I and our friends feel like nothing's going on. We came to the big city in the early nineties. Everything was pulsing. The clubs were full. Now it's dead. The air has gone out.

BG: In the seventies, all that energy went into sex and utopian politics.

IB: I wasn't around in the seventies . . . But I was at a political fund-raiser last week and I saw the mayor and all these national politicians looking into the fishbowl of gay life. I wondered what they thought . . . all that money, and energy, and talent . . . and not much focus.

BG: Gays might always have been a force driving spiritual life, dating back to the medieval monasteries and convents.

IB: Or to the shamans. Gays might even have a *special* spiritual gift . . . My partner and I have been planning to have two children. It costs about a hundred grand a child, with legal and medical costs.

BG: That's a commitment . . . but back to what you were saying before, someone once said that if all the gay ministers, organists, and choir directors didn't show up one Sunday, there'd be a great silence in Christendom.

IB: I'm more a Buddhist myself.

There are lots of dating manuals on the market. You can scroll down the list on any online bookstore and check new titles every few months: *Mr. Right Is Out There; Finding Your Leading Man; Finding True Love in a Man-Eat-Man World; Husband Hunting Made Easy.* What I haven't seen in the latest model of dating guide is a treatment of dating as a spiritual exercise. As I've confessed before, I've been burned many times in gay dating. But I've never encountered anything but respect and warmheartedness from anyone with whom I've been on a Socratic date. I guarantee: if you can move the conversation around to wisdom, you'll be more likely (in high school terms) to get to second base. If you can't, you might want to accept that there's not much of a future here.

Let Socrates be your guide. He dated himself in the tradition of the pre-Socratic philosopher Heraclitus, who summed up his search for wisdom as "I sought myself." Use your own Inner Oracle to get in touch with your own divine powers within. No one god is greater than another. Ideally, Apollo does not overpower Dionysus, Hermes, or Hephaestus. All must be balanced. To know them is to possess their powers. Then, like Socrates, use this self-knowledge to begin to get to know other more human heroes, or spiritual buddies. There will be a payoff. Remember that after all of the speeches about love have been spoken, *The Symposium* goes on for pages as we watch Alcibiades, the very embodiment of youth and beauty, doing his best to come on to the funny-looking, though obviously electric, Socrates.

The secret shared in *The Symposium*, perhaps the only dating guide you'll ever need, from Plato: Nothing is sexier than wisdom.

obviously practiced at putting some space around her thinking, said: "Feel the energy in the room. Feel the energy among us. We give thanks for being able to share in one another in this room. We are thankful for the questions of friends . . . both those who encourage us and those who try to restrain us."

By the time she spoke, I had finally spiraled deeply enough into my own private trance to manage to hear a message through the megaphone of my heart. As a spiritual tourist, I would have felt silly standing to share. And I can't say that the spirit behind the gnomic message I received wasn't Olympian rather than Quaker, if there is such a distinction: one of my decisions on the way over was not to overthink all this. My own personal telegram that day from the inner voice was humble enough: "Take it all in. Make the most of it."

As a clock in a tower somewhere outside in the cloudless blue sky struck noon, all who were present roused themselves from the contemplation of their own inner voices and of the inner voices raised by others. "Hello, good morning," said a young man next to me, shaking my hand, the only ritual of the entire service. All around me neighbors were greeting neighbors. Inspired—or as Socrates might have said, *retuned*—I exited the church of the Great Friend, dedicated centuries ago by its founder to the practice of listening to the inner voice.

SOCRATIC EXERCISES

1. Practice automatic writing.

2. Begin a daily practice of writing down a dialogue with your Voice Within.

3. Use the Voice Within as an Inner Oracle to discover your answers to the basic philosophical and spiritual questions of life and to identify your values.

4. Go on a date devoted to talking about life's big issues with an acquaintance, friend, or lover. Or insinuate a few moments of Socratic cross-examination into an ordinary conversation or online encounter.